ACCOMMODATING
THE LIVELY ARTS

An Architect's View
by Martin Bloom

Accommodating the Lively Arts

AN ARCHITECT'S VIEW
BY MARTIN BLOOM

SK

A Smith and Kraus Book

A Smith and Kraus Book
PO Box 127, Lyme, NH 03768

Copyright © 1997 by Martin Bloom
All rights reserved.
Cover and Text Design by Julia Hill/Freedom Hill Design
Illustrations © 1997 by Martin Bloom

Manufactured in the United States of America
First Edition: October 1997
10 9 8 7 6 5 4 3 2 1

The Library of Congress Cataloging-In-Publication Data
Bloom, Martin
Accommodating the lively arts: an architect's view / Martin Bloom. —1st ed.
p. cm. — (Career development series)
ISBN 1-57525-128-0
1. Theater architecture—United States. I. Title. II. Series.
NA6830.B66   1997
725'.822'0973—dc21   97-34439
CIP

AUTHOR

MARTIN BLOOM, Harvard-trained Architect and Urban Designer, has designed sets and lighting as well as performance facilities ranging from intimate chamber theatres seating fifty to spaces for large-scale performances accommodating thousands.

Since 1974, he has maintained an independent practice in New York City designing the Chelsea Theatre Manhattan project as well as developing *River, Trees, and Sea* (three demountable theatres designed for three specific sites) for Celebrate Brooklyn; the Theatre in Prospect Park; Repertory Theatre, Stony Point, N.Y. and the Midtown Satellite Theatre Museum for the Museum of the City of New York.

In recent years, he has planned laboratory theatre prototypes, regional cultural centers, theatre/commercial facility proposals for midtown Manhattan, a combination liturgical/ performance platform for St. Ann and the Holy Trinity in Brooklyn Heights, a series of demountable exhibition structures for trade shows including *Inforide*, and proposals for travelling museum exhibitions dealing with urban design.

Beginning in 1976 with an essay on the need for a more humanistic approach to theatre design, he has written a series of features on theatres and theatre districts for the *Journal of the American Institute of Architects* and for its successor, *Architecture*.

Contents

FOR R. W. B.

Introduction

by Charles Marowitz

One of the best-kept secrets in the theatre is the frequency with which architectural design totally frustrates the intentions of artists for whom such work is ostensibly undertaken. It is one of the theatre's greatest ironies that those who design its stages and auditoria, no matter how distinguished they may be as architects, are very often baboons when it comes to creating a space in which actors and audience can happily cohabit.

This shouldn't be surprising. Architects have rarely had to make quick changes or rapid entrances, throw their voices from the orchestra to the gallery, negotiate the interstices of backstage, wings and dressing rooms in frantic attempts to "make cues" or sustain the progress of a dramatic action. For an actor, a theatre is a domicile, a set of fixed parameters which he learns to negotiate as instinctively as he does the stairs, cellars and hallways of his own home. For an architect, it is often a monument to his ingenuity, a "spatial concept," an easel on which he can impose an original combination of planes and surfaces.

A few years back, I was involved in the creation of a new theatre complex in Los Angeles. Or to be more accurate, I was recruited onto the staff of a theatre complex which had already been created. There were four stages, one of them with an auditorium so steep you felt you needed mountain-climbing equipment to achieve your seat, another with a cozy thrust stage which loomed asymmetrically out into the house, making it impossible for a director to find a centerpoint for his mise-en-scène. The third was utterly conventional and the fourth, a so-called "black box" but one which aesthetically resisted the permutations for which black boxes are usually created. It would be an exaggeration to say the complex was a mess, but it certainly left a lot to be desired. It was the work of private architects working with only minimal input from the artists who were ultimately to inhabit the spaces and, like many such endeavors, it came into being with a slew of unsatisfactory compromises.

In an ideal situation, a theatre space is the physical embodiment of the ideas of the director or directors who are planning to work there. In the nonideal situation which usually obtains in the case of new theatres, it is a recycling of conventional practices by persons who base their ideas on received notions of theatre design. The disparity between theatrical expertise and architectural ingenuity is often very great and there is a tacit assumption that the architect's job is to build and the artist's to perform and, not only do the twain never meet, they never even need to.

That fatal dichotomy does not exist in the book you are presently holding in your hands because the author has approached the subject of theatre design from a pragmatic rather than a rigorously aesthetic standpoint. Or to put it more succinctly, Martin Bloom realizes that the only architectural design worth its salt is one that proceeds from a knowledge of performance dynamics. He concerns himself with the experience of acting and the experience of auditing, the incidence of sight and sound and how the interplay of all these elements can affect the quality of the event. He recognizes that the art of theatre is inextricable from questions of scope, timbre, proximity, and perception; that architecture is the handmaiden of theatre, not its despot, and that the theatre was made for man and not man for the theatre. These may seem obvious truths, but in practice, ones that are often neglected.

By lucidly surveying the innovations of the past centuries, he explains why we have come up with the stages we now possess and in so doing poses the question as to how they might change in the future. Aware that every problem requires its own individual solution, Bloom does not venture to prescribe a universal panacea, but his analyses and insights can help others focus on the elements they need to explore to find their particular way. Being a practical man of the theatre as well as an aesthetician, he concerns himself with mundane but essential matters such as legroom, sight lines, acoustics and assembly areas — making it clear that every factor that impinges upon comfort, audibility, and visibility affects an audience's perception of art.

As Bloom notes, when touring actors, moving rapidly from one city to another, arrive in a new theatre they often climb to the center of the stage, survey the auditorium and briskly clap their hands to judge the degree of resonance peculiar to that particular venue. In an instant, they can tell what visual and auditory problems they can expect to find once the audience assembles. They realize that the efficacy of their performance depends on a delicately determined ratio between the stage and the house. If theatre architects, using some comparable pragmatic means, were able to gauge these factors before they put pen to plans, the whole art of theatre design would be transformed.

It used to be said that theatre was nothing more than two planks and a passion, and in one sense that old saw remains true. The fact that those planks are now embossed in elaborate new textiles, swathed in a variety of rich upholstery and bolstered by the most technologically advanced equipment in the modern world doesn't alter the fact that it all exists for the sake of conveying that "passion."

Before the playwright has his script, the director his conception, the set-and-costume designers their sketches, or the actors their roles, the architect has spoken. Since it is his voice which precedes all the others, it behooves us to make sure that he knows what he is talking about. Theatre architecture is, of all the theatre arts, the one that most pressingly needs to be "accommodated" and this is precisely the service Martin Bloom has provided.

Foreword

This book is intended for all those who have ever experienced and derived pleasure from attending or participating in live performance. In these times, when the encroachment of simulated entertainment threatens the existence of live theatre, it is more important than ever to insure that the structures which house live performance be thoughtfully preserved and renovated and that new structures be wisely planned.

The development of performance spaces is a sometime activity, rare enough to warrant the closest attention whenever it occurs. Performance spaces, once built, tend to outlast their creators. Miscalculations made in one generation may haunt the users of the facilities through many subsequent generations. Therefore, this book is meant to help guide and stimulate the thinking of all those who might be involved in the planning of spaces for live performance — arts advocates, real estate developers, producers, directors, performers, educators, politicians, as well as city planners and architects. It is also intended for nonprofessionals who might one day find themselves serving on committees charged with the responsibility of developing new performing arts facilities or the renovation of existing ones.

What follows is an analysis of considerations that apply to the creation of most theatres: the importance of appropriate site selection; the cultural image that the theatre can project to the community; its management, sales, and control facilities; the efficiency of its lobbies and other front-of-the-house provisions; the characteristics of the stage together with its support system; and, above all, the crucial relationship between performers and audience.

To a greater or lesser degree, three underlying principles should inform the design of all theatres, from the most rudimentary to the most technically sophisticated:

(1) FOCUS — the capturing of an audience's attention by directing it toward an intended action

(2) PLATFORM — the provision of a marked-off performance location

(3) FRAME — the creation of an encompassing structure that may incorporate technical apparatus as well as define the environment of the performance.

The heart of theatre architecture lies in the establishment of a satisfactory relationship between those who perform and those who attend a performance. With this in mind, the role of continuing experimentation in relating audiences to performers is evaluated, with emphasis on how such experimentation might influence the evolution of new and meaningful architectural forms.

For those who are involved in the development of new theatre spaces or the preservation or adaptation of existing spaces, a consideration of contemporary needs combined with knowledge of the principles which have informed past theatrical solutions can assist in the creation of theatres appropriate for now and the future. These theatres, possibly designed in configurations which have never before existed, should be capable of responding to the evolving necessities of live performance, as theatre performance and theatre architecture move symbiotically into the next century.

ONE

Action...Reaction

We live in an age of technological wonders. Endless varieties of entertainments, once available only in theatres or concert halls, are ours at the touch of a button. Day or night, at home or abroad, on a beach or in a jet, we can summon up the sights and sounds of almost any conceivable performance whenever we are in the mood for it. Via film, tape, laser disc, and most recently as emanations of virtual reality from cyberspace, limitless entertainments lay themselves out before us through state-of-the-art speakers and screens.

Yet something essential is lacking in the experience when the performers of such entertainments do not share time and space with us during the event that is being transmitted. And how frustrating it is for us not to be able to express our reactions to their efforts on the spot and to encourage them on to even higher achievements. Simulations of performances, no matter how technically advanced, are at best frozen renderings of past accomplishments. Without direct contact, neither performers nor audiences can contribute to the vitality that only person-to-person live interaction can provide.

. . .

No configuration of pixels — no matter how convincingly "true-to-life" — can possibly match the impact of living performers on living audiences. When performances occur in real time within real space there is an exhilaration felt on both sides of the footlights that cannot be equalled. Performers who have been confined to working in recording studios or on sound stages for extended periods of time speak nostalgically about the rewards of performing before live audiences, where instantaneous response can goad them on to new heights of achievement. Similarly, when addicts of the home box venture out to sample entertainments presented in the flesh, they experience a high that hunkering down in front of a tube can never equal.

The interaction between performers and audience can ignite sparks which glow with unparalleled brilliance. Performers cannot help but be encouraged by the signals which come from an audience reacting positively to their performances. For an audience, urging performers on to the best of their capabilities and rewarding their achievements with commensurate demonstrations of approval can provide tremendous satisfaction. In fact, the ultimate success of any act of theatre —

whether it occurs within a formal enclave like Lincoln Center, or along Main Street, or on the side streets leading from Times Square or Piccadilly Circus — depends as much upon the degree of receptivity of a live audience as it does upon the talents of those on the stage.

. . .

An audience brings an indispensable ingredient to the theatrical event. It brings a contemporary consciousness. Theatre does not — in fact, *cannot* — exist in a vacuum. It reflects as well as modifies the world around it. In order to be truly effective, it must speak to an audience in ways that the audience can readily understand and it must be able to sustain an audience's attention for the duration of the performance. Achieving this is never easy. It requires as much talent, inspiration, and mastery of technique as the practitioner can muster. In short, it requires a deep understanding of what constitutes the "theatrical."

When people refer to something as "theatrical" what they usually imply is that something is overly extravagant or artificial. But that definition does not begin to do justice to the essence of theatre. At its best, theatre provides a heightened impression of life and gives it a degree of order and focus that, offstage, is usually absent. It is the mission of theatre to transform the frequently chaotic flow of existence into a sensible construct that audiences can react to and accept. Unlike life, where logic is rare and chaos rules, ideally, in theatre, events, concepts, and emotions are harnessed into a logical progression.

On the stage, events can frequently seem larger than life, wildly funny, or deeply affecting. The stage concentrates and intensifies life and raises it to a higher power. When live theatre succeeds, it blazes in ways that are unlike the ways achieved through any other medium. Theatre may have its highs and its lows, but, for those who perform in it and for those who attend it, it always provides immediacy and, under the right circumstances, a sense of occasion.

• • •

The idea of what constitutes the theatrical may appear to be a highly evolved notion, but it seems to have been grasped by performers from the very beginning. Even the most primitive performers understood that boring an audience was to be avoided at all costs. The Paleolithic hunter-turned-raconteur, relating the events of his day to his companions, must have felt it necessary to edit and synthesize his personal experiences. To prevent his audience from dozing or wandering off, he must have intuited the need to transcend the limitations of actuality — and possibly even to embellish the truth in order to entertain. A bald retelling of experience simply could not satisfy an ever-more-demanding audience. He had to employ art — or at the very least artifice — to enliven his interpretation of reality. His task was not only to perform but to rearrange facts with entertainment value in mind. And so, with an inventive, creatively inspired teller of a tale, theatre was born.

The demands of effective performance, however, eventually required more than a solo — no matter how compelling that solo might have been. Primitive man's descendants soon discovered that a story could be rendered more vividly by telling it according to several points of view. So dialogue superseded monologue, and one-person storytellers were replaced by small groups of individualized performers.

At first, these performers staged their events in open spaces, preferably on pre-existing stone threshing floors with spectators standing or squatting on all sides. In time, as casts of characters grew, so did the relative size of the audiences. Soon so many were attracted to the event that it became necessary to provide graduated levels for the spectators so that adequate sight lines to the performance could be achieved. This was most readily accomplished by positioning the performance circle at the base of a hill out of which could be carved concentric rows of seating rising up the slope in order to facilitate sight lines for theatres which eventually could accommodate whole communities. Tiring sheds, flanking the playing circle, provided the necessary concealed preparation areas for the performers and in time developed into the sort of stage and backstage support facilities with which we are familiar today.

When, over the course of centuries, theatre moved indoors, accommodations for spectators and performers were constantly being re-evaluated and modified. A delicate balance had to be struck over and over again between the demands of those performing and the demands of those coming to see and hear that performance. Sometimes the stage intruded into the heart of the auditorium; sometimes it retreated into a realm of its own behind an arch. At each point, the respective heights and slopes of platform and auditorium were readjusted relative to one another so that the arrangement could fulfill its essential obligation to the performer/audience relationship.

. . .

Even more than the form of a church, museum, sports stadium, library, or city hall, the form of a theatre expresses the cultural aspirations of the society that built it. The lobbies and promenades, the seating arrangements and their relationships to the stage reveal the social and economic forces that were at work at the time of each theatre's creation. Subsequent modifications to a theatre's original form mirror accommodations to changing times and circumstances and present a concise history of the evolution of the culture.

Autocratic or democratic, the theatre is a place where people can congregate to experience life in a form more focussed, comprehensible, and heightened than in day-to-day existence. It is meant to house an artistic distillation of the human condition rendered in terms of movement and speech, song and dance, color and light. How well the ideas developed on stage are communicated to the audience depends to a very large extent on the design of the theatre — the physical structure in which that communication unfolds.

Live performance, unlike prerecorded television and film, makes unusually complicated demands on performers and spectators. For one thing, it happens on the moment and there is no possibility for subsequent editing, dubbing, or retakes. The effectiveness of a particular performance is determined by its reception in the immediate here and now. Theatre therefore demands a high degree of alertness on the part of both performer and perceiver. Action begets reaction — instantaneously. And the success or failure of that action and that reaction are, in no small part, dependent on the spaces in which these actions and reactions take place.

The physical arrangement of a theatre — in a word, its architecture — can either enhance or detract from the efforts to create a satisfactory live experience. At the very least, performers should be able to project to an audience without strain; for its part, the audience should be able to see, hear, and respond readily to the impulses being directed toward it.

A well-designed theatre should facilitate an unfettered flow of energy back and forth within whatever spatial arrangement has been devised to accommodate performers and audience. A well-designed theatre should also be able, at the proper moment, to unite these components into a totality that fulfills the ultimate potential of the live event. It should be capable of bestowing an aura of the extraordinary on the merely human. It should so focus attention on the event unfolding within its precincts that the audience released from the concerns of the mundane, becomes, for the "two hours' traffick of the stage," completely involved in the unfolding theatrical reality.

Such daunting requirements conspire to rank theatres among the most difficult building types to deal with in all of architecture. A formal aesthetic that can encompass so complex an array of functional demands is elusive at best. It is no wonder that many of the more conscientious practitioners of every age have frequently shied away from the challenge of creating workable theatres. It is also no wonder that when virtuoso

designers, unconcerned with the practical aspects of the theatrical event and intent on producing eye-catching solutions
at all costs, tackle the occasional theatre, the results may be satisfying to them and to their personal aesthetic, but are often
far less satisfying to the performers and audiences forced to
cope with the consequences of such frequently misguided self-
indulgence. The sheer number of requirements necessary to
facilitate adequate performance and witnessing is staggering,
and the synthesis of all these into an aesthetic and functional
whole often tests the limits of human ingenuity.

But, through the centuries, whenever theatrical performance has enjoyed wide appeal, there has been no lack of individuals — royal, ecclesiastical, municipal, or entrepreneurial
— eager to sponsor places for its presentation. And so there
have also been those intrepid enough to accept the challenge
of designing appropriate structures to contain live performed
events. The result is a long tradition of theatre building that,
if properly understood, can inspire and inform our contemporary efforts to provide physical settings to support and
enhance live performance — and, in so doing, give the incom-
parable value of face-to-face live theatre a stunning advantage
over the all-too-available and often debilitating virtual reality
"entertainments" of our day.

However, before we delve into the past in search of the
light it might possibly cast on solutions appropriate to our particular needs, it is important that we be able to identify the
categories of physical components basic to all theatres.
Accordingly, the following chapter deals with the essential
characteristics of the places and spaces that make up any per-

forming arts facility regardless of specific size, shape, actor/ audience configuration or cultural context.

TWO

Places and Spaces

No matter how well designed a theatre may be — no matter how efficiently its structure may facilitate the flow of energy back and forth from performer to audience — if it is not built in a suitable location it might just as well not have been built at all. Too many otherwise satisfactory theatres have languished for lack of audience simply because they were built in the wrong place.

The producer and developer Oscar Hammerstein, grand-father of the future lyricist and librettist of *Show Boat*, *Oklahoma!* and *The Sound of Music*, was celebrated among his peers for his knack of choosing the worst possible sites for his theatres. For this late 19th century Manhattan impresario, bankruptcy followed bankruptcy. Then, in 1899, he sensed an opportunity when he anchored 42nd Street and Seventh Avenue with his new Victoria Theatre. The result was highly successful and, as other entrepreneurs followed suit, his inspiration led directly to the development of the theatre block on 42nd Street and subsequently to the launching of the Times Square entertainment phenomenon.

Not every theatre developer, however, was as fortunate as Hammerstein. Many who guessed wrong about where to locate their enterprises never recovered from the miscalculation. The history of theatre building is littered with examples of splendidly crafted houses closing after a few financially disastrous seasons. The wrong neighborhood, the wrong street, even the wrong side of the street — any or all of these factors could spell ruin for many otherwise prudent entrepreneurs.

· · ·

It is impossible to overestimate the decisive influence site selection has on the ultimate success or failure of any theatre, no matter how well that theatre might otherwise have been designed. There are as many examples of substandard facilities doing well in choice locations as there are examples of superior ones struggling to survive simply because they were built in the wrong place. Location can make a major economic difference. In New York City, the stylistically distinguished Lyceum Theatre and the technically advanced Belasco have frequently remained dark only because they were unfortunate enough to have been built to the east of Broadway while many of their less satisfactory contemporaries to the west of Broadway continue to be profitably booked year in and year out.

The context — urban or rural — of any proposed theatre should be carefully considered at the very beginning of the planning process. As a product of the culture that spawns it, a theatre is a place of public assembly and cannot thrive in a vacuum. It will occupy a specific position on a particular street in a particular part of town and will partake of the characteristics of that location. The environmental atmosphere of its surround becomes part of the very fabric of the playhouse and helps to define its character.

Therefore, every attempt should be made to establish a healthy symbiotic relationship between a theatre and its immediate surroundings. Complementary elements such as galleries, shops, restaurants, and cafés lend vitality to the area and, if they do not already exist, should be incorporated into any contemplated scheme. In an urban context, theatres can act as powerful generators of activity, but when they are dark — as they sometimes are — other elements must be available to take up the slack and contribute to keeping the area alive.

. . .

No matter where a theatre is situated, it should, at the very least, be easily accessible. There should be ample and convenient parking for those who come by car, proximity to public transportation for those who use that method, and a pleasant, secure environment for pedestrians once they have arrived. If the ambience surrounding the theatre happens to be festive enough to create a mood of anticipation for the event to come, so much the better.

The approach to a theatre should set the tone for the experience. The marquee should project and protect and announce. It should beckon, welcome, and lure. After dark, it should dazzle with light. Like the cover of a book, it should hint at what awaits within.

Beneath the marquee are located the entranceways which admit us to the attraction. Ample enough to accommodate preperformance and exiting crowds, they should be easy to negotiate. On either side can be the images that evoke the specific event — the signs, posters, photos, and quotations from press reviews. The facade of the theatre should be designed so as to act as a slate on which the current production may be announced dynamically, but the permanent aspects of the building's essential character should never be overwhelmed. In other words, the house should maintain its identity while graciously allowing self-expression to its transient guests.

Just beyond the entranceways, the box office area should be allotted sufficient space so that lines of ticket buyers do not impede the flow of those already ticketed and entering the theatre itself. For convenience, there should ideally be at least three designated box office positions — previously sold reservations, current sale, and advance sale — with sufficient access and queuing space for each. Overhead and conveniently visible should be some form of seating diagram with up-to-the-moment data concerning availabilities for current and future performances. For the patrons, everything possible should be done to make the ticket-buying process as efficient and enjoyable as possible.

Accessible from the outer lobby, but in a comparatively inconspicuous location, there should be a clearly marked entrance to the administration area. Here the staff and management of the theatre have their offices. Those having business here should be able to come and go without having to enter the theatre itself.

There should be sufficient space in the outer lobby to allow for discreet circulation paths so that congestion before and after performances may be kept to a minimum. Space should be allotted away from these paths of circulation for patrons not yet ready to enter the theatre or who may be waiting for companions to join them. The lighting level should be bright enough so that the ticketing and control functions leading to the interior of the theatre can be efficiently handled. The outer lobby space, while it must be businesslike and efficient, nevertheless serves as a prelude to the whole theatre-going experience and should be sensitively devised to enhance anticipation for the event to come.

• • •

As one approaches the entrance to the inner lobby and passes through the control — surrendering one's ticket and receiving a stub that indicates the location one will occupy during the event itself — one should begin to sense one's relationship to the theatre as a whole. The locations of checking facilities, rest rooms, and public telephones should be immediately apparent, and the most direct pathway to that particular portion of the theatre where one will eventually be seated should be unambiguous and clear.

Having unburdened oneself of coats and parcels, one should be able to move freely into the highly structured environment which little by little will prepare one for the event to come. If there is time to wander, there should be interesting things to contemplate — perhaps images of past events in this theatre, perhaps something of the history of the building itself or the cultural climate that brought it about. Elements that link the current production to some larger context will enhance the effectiveness of the impending event.

To facilitate social interaction, the space of the lobby should be ample enough to enable a capacity audience to circulate freely before and after a performance and during intermissions. Adding to the conviviality of the scene in this area should be a counter for the serving of drinks and snacks.

Although ordinarily accessible only to theatre patrons, the main lobby is an interior version of a public space and should be designed as such. If it is possible to provide glimpses of the immediate surroundings through window openings or through doors leading onto terraces, courtyards, or even enclosed gardens, a variety of experiences can be achieved that will add to the dynamics of the space and contribute a visual and aesthetic amenity.

If the size of the lobby can approximate the size of the playing area on the main stage, it might be possible for the space to be used for rehearsals when the stage itself is unavailable for this purpose. And if the dimensions of the lobby could permit this magnitude of function, it might easily accommodate any number of other uses such as conferences, exhibitions, commercial demonstrations, receptions, fundraisers, and all sorts of social events that might add considerably to the revenues of the theatre.

In addition, the lobby might be designed to convert to an after-performance cabaret. In this case, the food facilities already provided might service this function as well, and portable tables and chairs, conveniently stored, could accommodate a separately ticketed audience. A small, strategically placed platform, sufficiently raised for good sight lines and provided with theatrical lighting, could become the focus for the cabaret entertainment, and the dressing rooms of the theatre could double as preparation space for the performers who would appear.

Anything that can support the financial well-being of a theatre in addition to subscriptions and individual ticket sales is of vital importance to the stability of the institution and suitable facilities should be provided wherever possible. For example, an adjacent theatre memorabilia and bookstore might prove useful not only for the sales that it could generate but for the cultural image it could project to the community as a whole. Museums have found such facilities to be immensely profitable and, if creatively stocked and promoted, so can theatres.

The size and complexity of a lobby is dependent, of course, on the size and complexity of the theatre that it serves. If the capacity of the theatre is to be relatively large, the seating might have to be arranged on a number of levels. The requisite stairways, elevators, and ramps needed to support such an arrangement might reasonably be reflected within the space of the lobby and contribute to its character. There might be viewing positions from each of these levels overlooking the main lobby and the height and breadth of the space might be correspondingly monumental.

Whether large or small, a lobby establishes the mind-set for the ensuing event. As a place in which to see and be seen — as a setting for a form of social theatre in which the spectator becomes the performer — a lobby can assist in transforming the ticketholder into an alert participant in the event about to take place within the theatre itself. It's not that the audience will be expected to participate alongside the performers — at least not in the conventional sense — unless, of course, such is the intention of the production. But, aided by the ambience of the lobby, the individual members of the audience can be transformed into that most prized component of a theatrical event — an assembly of expectant, attentive, and responsive witnesses to what is about to transpire just beyond the doors to the auditorium.

• • •

As one approaches the entrance to the auditorium, one should proceed through a transitional zone in which the lighting and sound levels of the lobby are gradually diminished. In addition to adjusting one's senses to the precisely controlled conditions one will encounter in the auditorium, such light and sound locks act as barriers to protect the house from outside distractions and are essential to maintaining the integrity of the event.

Once inside the auditorium, one should be able to take the measure of the totality of the space and to judge one's relationship to it. The ability to comprehend this at a glance is essential to developing a sense of security within an unfamiliar environment. The lighting level, somewhat diminished from that of the lobby, should nonetheless be bright enough to allow one to follow an usher with confidence along aisles or down ramps to one's assigned position in the hall.

Having been conducted to the row containing one's assigned location, one should be able to negotiate the space between the rows and get to one's seat without undue inconvenience either to oneself or one's immediate neighbors. The seat itself, clearly identified by letter and number to correspond to one's ticket stub, should be comfortable, with enough height, width, and elbow room to accommodate a wide range of physical types. There should also be enough legroom and sufficient space to allow others to be able to pass without too much difficulty. In addition, provision should be made for convenient wheelchair access to clearly marked locations distributed evenly throughout the auditorium without compromising sight lines for any portion of the audience.

Once seated, there should be enough ambient light so that one can grasp the size, shape, and appearance of the room. It is extremely disconcerting for theatregoers to find themselves awaiting the start of a performance while seemingly afloat in a dark and undefined space. The colors and textures of walls and ceiling should relate harmoniously to the seating areas and tie the whole composition of the room into a cohesive whole.

Such considerations heighten the sense of security and anticipation for an audience adjusting to an unfamiliar environment.

In addition to the ambient illumination that gives the space its character, narrowly focussed downlighting should be provided for all seating areas so that programs may be read with ease. Also, aisles and exits should be precisely lit and readily identifiable during performances without distracting from the event itself.

The focus for the auditorium arrangement, of course, lies within the performance space and seating should be arranged to accommodate that focus. It cannot be stressed too strongly: The ability of an audience to see and to hear is the prime motivating force behind the design of any auditorium. Sight lines and acoustics are essential considerations, and seating positions and floor slopes all must be carefully calculated for optimal visual and auditory access.

The requirements of an audience — that it be able to see and hear the performance with ease — might be assumed to be taken for granted were it not for how often these considerations are handled without any real conviction in actual theatres. The myriad possibilities for achieving workable actor/audience relationships will be analyzed in subsequent chapters. For now let it be said that these arrangements — the relationships between performers and audience — constitute the heart of theatre design.

Located within the auditorium space, but for the exclusive use of the production, are lighting and sound positions and a control booth with an unobstructed view of the performance space. Although physically present, these facilities should be incorporated as much as possible into the architecture of the room and be as unobtrusive to the audience as possible. Equally unobtrusive should be a system of ventilation, humidity and temperature control for the entire space that is efficient enough and silent enough not to impinge on an audience's concentration.

As the time for the event nears, individual members of the audience, settled in their separate locations, will begin to focus their attention on the performance space and, as they do, become a coherent and attentive body ready to react to the stimuli of the production. As the house lights dim, the environment of the audience space gradually loses its identity and begins to yield to the reality of the stage.

• • •

A stage is, ideally, a strategically crafted void capable of receiving and accommodating whatever modifications of space and light a particular production might require. Under appropriate circumstances, it allows the presentation of a heightened reality — more focussed, more persuasive than anything that can be experienced outside a theatre. When filled with a creative presentation, this atmosphere bonds a collection of individual spectators into an assembly which can remain unified for the duration of a theatrical event.

Actually, the development of such a state of high potential is achieved through very practical, physical, and down-to-earth means. Based, of course, on creative inspiration, the process depends on a complex blending of calculated effects determined by the production team, as the performers' portrayals are combined with the environmental sleight-of-hand of sets, costumes, and lights. Supporting all of this performance "magic" is the very practical world of precise space and technology known as the backstage. This area, ordinarily off-limits to the public, is governed by its own rules of organization and procedure. Since equipment within it is both expensive and potentially dangerous for the uninitiated, access to it is strictly controlled. Security is the key.

Arrival and departure of authorized personnel, material and equipment is monitored. There should be well-defined areas to accommodate the various functions that contribute to the event. If the sets, costumes, and props are fabricated on site, there must be separate and adequate shop space allocated for each of these categories. If these production elements are fabricated off-site, there must be trucking access via a loading dock and secure storage space provided within easy access of the stage.

If at all possible, there should be provision for rehearsal space in the backstage area equal to the actual stage space. Sometimes this can be accomplished by positioning the rehearsal space directly beneath the stage itself, allowing the structure for the substage to reflect identical dimensions. This space can also serve as below-stage access to stage-level floor traps if needed. It can also be used as a preparation area for musicians, with direct access to the orchestra pit, and as a mass dressing room for chorus members and supernumeraries.

Dressing rooms should be arranged for maximum practicality and comfort. There should be secure lockers for street clothes and personal possessions. There should be adequate open hanging space for costumes with convenient access to toilets and showers. There should be provisions for privacy and the separation of sexes. Floors, walls, and dressing tables should be surfaced with materials that can be easily maintained. Mirrors over dressing tables should be free of distortion and surrounded by lighting that can approximate the intensities on stage. Full-length mirrors should be wide enough and tall enough to completely reflect the costumed performer. Access from the dressing areas to the stage should be convenient, direct, and well-lighted.

It is important that all areas be linked by intercom with each other and with the stage itself. During performance, sounds on stage should be broadcast continuously throughout the backstage area and in individual dressing rooms so that all those connected with the production can hear the performance and be ready in time for their participation in the event.

A greenroom, comfortably outfitted with easy chairs and couches for relaxation, and providing vending machines and facilities for simple food preparation, should be adjacent to the dressing area and convenient to the stage. Here performers may run their lines, unwind during rehearsals, or await their cues to appear on stage. The greenroom is also a place where they can meet and socialize with an invited public after a performance and therefore it should be reachable via a relatively inconspicuous route from the house.

In general, the paths which performers take and which members of the audience take in order to perform their individual functions are separated from each other. The spectator is kept outside the realm of the purveyors of the "magic." During rehearsals, links between the auditorium and backstage are often useful. During performance, however, these links are usually disguised to discourage patrons from intruding on the performers' turf. Similarly, the venerable stage door, with its custodian, is available for the actors and crew to make their entrances and exits from the theatre without having to traverse the audience area.

All access from backstage to the stage should be direct and convenient for technicians as well as for performers. Paths of circulation should permit scenic elements to move to and from the stage without inhibiting the movements of the cast. The two patterns of flow — performers and set pieces — should be complementary to, and independent of, each other and the space available adjacent to the stage should be adequate to accommodate this. All evidence of light and sound emanating from the backstage area should be suitably masked so that the audience is not distracted from the onstage performance.

· · ·

Basically, the stage itself is a floor or platform ample enough to accommodate the ground plan of any given production. While this updated "threshing floor" could be any size, as a general rule an unencumbered space approximately 40 feet wide by 40 feet deep should be able to accommodate any sort of performance, from the simplest drama to the most complicated opera or ballet. The blocking or the choreography of any presentation should be able to be handled within such a playing area as long as sufficient wing and cross-over space is allotted around the active area to allow access of performers and scenic elements at any point along the periphery.

The stage floor itself should be designed with sufficient spring to insure a safe and efficient dance surface. If built to dance specifications, it will automatically serve any other form of production. If possible, the floor should be divisible into removable sections to permit traps at any position, allowing a full range of entrances from below-stage.

Built-in revolves, treadmills, sliding platforms, and stage elevators — although useful for quick set changes and special effects — tend to inhibit the flexibility of a stage and the possibility of a full trapping of the floor. Generally speaking, such devices are best employed on a production-to-production basis and may be installed over the stage floor temporarily, with filler platforms to maintain a flush performance surface.

Immediately adjacent offstage areas — wing spaces and upstage cross-overs — should be ample enough to accommodate set pieces and performers awaiting their appearances on stage. As a rule, half the width of the stage opening on each side provides an adequate wing arrangement for an arched stage. If, for example, the width of the stage opening is 40 feet, then twenty feet on each side is a convenient solution and can also accommodate quick-change facilities for cast members unable to reach and return from their dressing rooms in the allotted time.

For stages where scenery is to be raised and lowered, there should be fly space directly over the stage and wing areas rising at least two and a half to three times the height of the play-ing space. Just below the roof should be an accessible grid from which regularly spaced parallel pipes are suspended on coun-terweighted lines. These pipes support lights, drops, travellers, and dimensional scenic elements. They can be raised and low-ered mechanically according to production need.

Sets of vertical light poles should be positioned on the sides within the wing spaces to provide onstage side lighting. Overhead light pipes covering the entire stage area at regular intervals should permit complete down- and backlighting. These, combined with light positions aimed at the stage from within the audience area, should be sufficient to cover all fore-seeable illumination requirements for any type of performance.

To accommodate musical performances, an orchestra pit may be required. This may take the form of a permanent open gulf separating the audience from the stage or there might be provisions for the occasional removal of portions of the for-ward edge of the stage floor. Either solution would permit the placement of musicians below stage level in order not to inter-fere with audience sight lines, but would also allow the con-ductor an unobstructed view of the performance on stage.

In the case of a proscenium theatre, the forestage may be designed as an elevator which can sink to form an orchestra pit when required. In addition, the proscenium frame itself may be mechanically adjustable in order to modify the height and width of the stage opening depending upon production demand.

. . .

As noted before, the relationship of the performance space to the audience space is at the core of theatre architecture. The requirements of each are complex and demand a high level of precision in design and execution. Neither can exist independently. The arrangement of one is totally dependent on its relationship to the other. They coexist in a delicate balance which, if it works, can provide the vessel for a satisfactory live theatrical experience.

Regardless of the configuration of the audience area, the stage must act as a focus of attention for all of the individual spectators who make up the audience. To achieve this, the stage must be high enough and prominent enough to be seen by everyone in the house and shaped so that any scenic elements supporting the performers may be grasped as a totality in performance.

When a performer stands stage center, he or she can generally judge the effectiveness of the theatre by surveying the auditorium. If the performer can see all the seats at a glance without much head movement side to side or up and down, there is a good chance that he or she will be in a position to command the attention of the entire audience. If the performer then claps hands and doesn't hear a discernible echo, chances are that he or she will not have to strain to be heard.

The ability of a performer to gauge the reactions of an audience is every bit as significant as the ability of an audience to see and hear a performance. The success of a live theatrical event is dependent on mutual interaction. If nuances of sight and sound must be communicated, a performance will suffer if a house is too large or too rangy. In the case of opera or ballet or ballet or musicals or the extravaganzas that fill mammoth venues such as Radio City Music Hall, the overall impact of performance is not usually dependent on subtlety of nuance. The outsized stylization of the production is calculated to overcome the great distances involved in accommodating vast audiences. In this case, reaction to the performance is magnified by the sheer size of the audience as it responds en masse to meet the energy of the larger-than-life performance being projected from the stage.

In a theatre for live spoken performance, however, achieving the effect of intimacy, regardless of the physical size of the house, is of the greatest importance. An accomplished actor, armed with exceptional talent and secure interpretive techniques, is sometimes able to overcome inadequacies in the architecture of a theatre space. Others, however, not so fortunately endowed, may fare less well. As a result, from the audience's point of view, the overall performance may suffer. A poorly designed theatre will not support the total intention of the theatrical event and will be a source of frustration to the performer as well as to the audience. A well-designed theatre, on the other hand, will enhance performers and performances at all levels and, while not guaranteeing excellence in the communication, will, at least, give that communication its best chance.

As the house lights dim at the start of a performance, the individual members of the audience, fixed in their assigned positions, begin to focus on the performance space. As the curtain rises or, on a curtainless stage, when the stage lights reach their intended intensity, those individuals immediately begin to judge whether or not they will be in a position to see with ease the full dimensions of the playing area.

For the majority of individuals to feel comfortable with their physical relationship to the stage, the seating arrangement must complement the stage space, and the sight lines from each individual position to the stage must be clear and unimpeded. If, when the performers begin to move and speak, the individual audience members can see and hear with clarity and comprehension, the balance between these two disparate worlds has been achieved.

Actors and directors tend to think of themselves as confronting or being surrounded by a *body* of observers. From the audience's point of view, however, each person is looking at the event through his or her own eyes. Separately. If each individual can see and hear everything that the production intends to project, then these individuals are well on their way to becoming an assembly capable of reacting as a unit. When such a phenomenon occurs, the performers immediately sense it and are able to communicate with confidence and concentrate on giving their very best to the event. If, however, some of the individual members of the audience are prevented from responding with the group because they are unable to see or hear all of the proceedings, the response will be fragmented. The performers will sense this as well and the fullest potential of the performance will not be reached.

A successful theatrical event is a cooperative endeavor, with the audience contributing responsively to the performance. The energy generated under proper circumstances arcs continuously from performers to spectators and back again so that the air is charged with a palpable level of excitement. In such a situation, anything is possible and, if the performance is of sufficient quality, both sides can then experience a rare and mutual feeling of exhilaration. The configuration of a theatre can aid or inhibit such a phenomenon. The potential for this sort of dynamic communication is dependent upon the physical accommodation that the structure provides.

The term "theatre" is a noun which refers both to the structure in which a performance takes place and to the performance itself. When people say "That is good theatre" we assume they are talking about a production. When they say "That is *a* good theatre" we assume they are talking about the space in which that production occurs. These may seem to be two different concepts but, in fact, they are totally wedded. The structure and the performance which unfolds within it are intricately intertwined. It is important, therefore, to be able to explore the varieties of structures that can be created to house theatre.

As there are many varieties of performances (theatre), so there are many varieties of structures (theatres). Different approaches to performance can suggest different arrangements in space and so many diverse designs have evolved through time that practitioners today may find themselves, with reason, confused by the ambiguities and inconsistencies expressed by these various solutions. To better evaluate the individual significance of these examples and to extract whatever relevance they may have for our particular needs, it is important to familiarize ourselves with the principles of Focus, Platform, and Frame. Their pivotal roles in influencing the various spatial solutions must be understood and appreciated. Only then will we be prepared to undertake the design of theatres appropriate to our particular time, place, and circumstance with full confidence in our abilities to further the cause of live performance.

THREE

Focus

Focus should play a major role in the design of all theatres. While it is more defining in the audience-encircling theatre-in-the-round, the principle of focus is essential to all forms of theatre.

The drawing of an audience's attention toward a performance is fundamental to the development of any theatre, regardless of its specific configuration. It is as if, in the midst of a gathering, certain individuals, inspired to "create spectacles of themselves," cause all ears to focus on their words and all eyes on their actions. From the very beginning, facilitating such concentration and finding ways of sustaining it have been on-going preoccupations of those whose aim it is to design useful theatres.

From archeological evidence dating back to prehistory, we find variations on arrangements featuring a central performance area meant to be encircled by standing or squatting spectators. Early performers, in search of appropriate performance locations, opted for flat, open spaces and found the occasional pre-existing stone threshing floor, with its circular shape and flat surface, convenient for their purposes.

The primitive, essentially nondirectional performance space surrounded by an audience still plays a significant role in our contemporary theatre. Clearly more people can get closer to an event this way than by ranging themselves on only one, two, or three sides. This, plus the fact that so little scenic investiture seems necessary to support such a performance, is the major justification for its continued use.

. . .

Except for the occasional remains of a threshing floor, there are no examples of purely central stages surviving from antiquity. However, there do exist a number of relatively recent interpretations of this form. Many are to be found in colleges and universities where economics and simplicity of production figure significantly in the choice of theatre form and where, in one complex, there might also be several other configurations and capacities of theatres. Some studio theatres in England, namely the Royal Exchange Theatre in Manchester, have a central focus. And in the United States, examples of theatres-in-the-round have been developed at the Penthouse Theatre in Seattle, Washington, the original Alley Theatre in Houston, Texas, and the large capacity Casa Mañana in Ft. Worth, Texas.

Any performance space — anywhere, anytime — must first facilitate the possibility of focussing all attention on the event to be staged within it. The audience should be arranged so that it can see, hear, and react as a unit to impulses being directed toward it from an established point of concentration.

Performers, working from this point of concentration, must be enabled to freely assert their right to command the audience's attention. "Observe what we do! Heed what we say ... and react!"

Attracted to an event, an audience congregates, pressing in as closely as possible — the better to see, the better to hear.

Calibrating their senses to the sights and sounds of a particular perfor-
mance while discounting the effect of any environmental distractions,
an audience bonds with a performer to create the possibility for recip-
rocal interaction.

A focus is established.

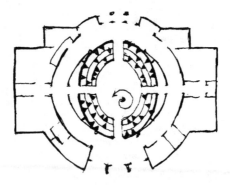

Installed within an enclosure and isolated from the influence of sun or
rain or time of day, focus is reinforced.

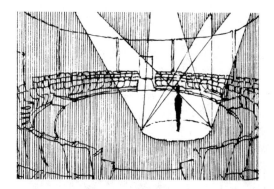

In an intimate, neutral environment, such as the one shown here (Penthouse Theatre, Seattle, Washington), surrounded by rows of seats on graduated levels and with controllable overhead lighting, all eyes and ears can more readily be concentrated on a planned event.

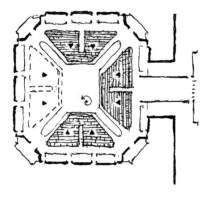

In a larger facility, such as the Arena Stage in Washington, D. C., seen above, audience access is physically separated from that of the performer and an even greater impression of performance focus can be established and maintained.

*With catwalks for the installation of flexible lighting and a grid for fly-
ing scenic elements above and floor traps for below-stage entrances, focus
is made palpable in architectural terms and its dominance is reinforced
by state-of-the-art technical support.*

*From a clearing in the woods to a high-tech enclosed performance
facility, the human body in space is the focus for an encircling audience.*

While many extant central stages exist as improvisations
in found spaces like warehouses, factories, and gymnasiums,
the Arena Stage in Washington, D. C. has been housed since
the early 1960s in a structure designed and built to its own
specifications. These specifications, however, evolved over an
eleven-year period of experimentation conducted first in a
derelict movie house and subsequently in a converted brew-
ery. This latter incarnation of 500 seats provided the basis for
the program that informed the design of the much-expanded
and technically refined present structure.

Surrounding a flat, central, slightly more rectangular than square performance area are four seating sections of eight rows each rising up from the stage level and backed by a series of boxes arranged beyond an encircling aisle. The seating capacity is slightly over 800 and the arrangement of risers and aisles permits an intimate involvement between performers and spectators. Four entrance tunnels, one at each corner of the performance space, permit onstage access, and a ceiling grid provides a flexible arrangement of lights.

Although the concept has here been sensitively rendered as a virtually neutral elongated cube, it is interesting to notice that one of the four surrounding seating sections — the one opposite the entrance lobby — has been designed as a removable bleacher to permit three-sided staging if some form of elevated scenic background should be required. In most productions, however, this modification has been resisted because it tends to diminish the intended effect of theatre-in-the-round and, more significantly, because it cuts down the audience capacity to a less economical level.

The principal challenge of the central staging form involves a critical balance between the frontality of performers and their complete encirclement by spectators. It is obvious that the effect of facial expressions crucial to a dramatic intention is confined only to those members of an audience who can actually see an actor's face at any particular moment. In central staging, at any one moment part of the audience might be seeing two actors in profile, part might be seeing both of their backs, part might be seeing the face of one and the back of another, while the audience on the opposite side of the stage might be experiencing the back of the first and the face of the second. This tends to fragment an audience's reaction.

Of course, one actor's facial expressions might be relayed to the rest of the audience by the faces of other actors reacting to him. However, in an effort to reach all members of an encircling audience, there is a tendency for actors to move in circular or spiral patterns, thereby slowing the overall pace of the performance and conveying the effect of waltzing mice. Ironically, the more a director feels obligated to communicate with all sections of an audience equally, the more this effect occurs.

However, when a director, either from lack of time, talent or energy, loses sight of the necessity to play to the entire encircling audience and directs the rehearsals from a single fixed position in the auditorium, another equally vexing situation arises. The needs of three-quarters of the audience are abandoned. They are left to view principally the backs and sides of the actors and, as the performance continues, they begin to feel alienated from the event.

A production of Strindberg's *Dance of Death* which I attended at the Arena Stage illustrates this phenomenon. From my seat opposite the lobby side of the theatre, the performance of the first act seemed strangely remote considering the intimate proportions of the space. I gradually realized that the furniture on stage had been arranged as though it were installed on a one-sided stage facing the opposite direction. When I changed seats at intermission and viewed the second act from the opposite side, I was far more involved in the action. It was a completely different experience from my viewing of the first act.

One of the major inducements for building many central stage theatres is that such an arrangement usually minimizes the need for elaborate physical setting. To accommodate the surrounding audience's sight lines, low-backed chairs and tables on carpets, or benches and tree stumps on patterned ground cloths are about all that can be permitted on stage. On the other hand, requirements for lighting in the round can be enormous for, no matter which way performers face, they must have a light source which will illuminate their features for that particular segment of the audience.

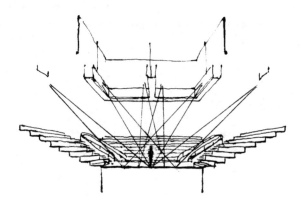

Since spectators are seated all around the performance area, the front of an actor must be lighted from positions covering 360 degrees around any acting position on the stage.

An audience encircling a central performance focus must be enabled to observe without hindrance all significant aspects of any given production. Since the performers must communicate to such an audience with comparable impact for all sides, overhead lighting positions must allow every acting location to be independently illuminated from at least four sources...with angles of incidence kept within the strictest bounds to minimize glare.

Central-focus staging primarily depends on the expressive use of actors in space. Aided by costuming and a minimum of props, it is the in-the-round performer who must carry the burden of the dramatic intention from moment to moment.

Vertical atmospheric enhancements such as walls or screens can play no significant part here. Furnishings taller than tabletops or low-backed chairs may obscure audience sightlines. Any enclosures required by the script should be transparent or skeletonized and struck as soon as possible. Only the floor and possibly an abstraction of a ceiling can intrude on what is essentially a transparent performance space defined by an encircling auditorium.

Transforming such space into a scenic interior is generally accomplished by covering the performance floor with carpeting or a cloth patterned to suggest a specific type of interior flooring. Furnishings, carefully chosen to evoke the particular ambience of the scene, are arranged to support and modify the movements of the actors with due attention being paid to audience sight lines.

An impression of vertical enclosure is sometimes suggested by a framework of ceiling beams or an occasional chandelier suspended from above but so positioned as not to interfere with the functioning of over-head production lighting. Door frames, if physically necessary for the production, should be placed in the entranceways well beyond the range of audience sight lines onto the principal action.

Exterior settings tend to be more abstract. Here, actual pieces of furniture which give an immediate sense of scale to an interior play a far less significant role. Of course, benches, stumps, and outcrops of rock which can support the actors and the action provide that scale but, more often, it is the floor treatment depicting soil, sand, pavement, or grass that suggests

the exact location. Also, suspended elements such as branches or banners,
arranged so as not to interfere with area lighting, can sculpt and define
the intended environment.

However, in the central-focus form, the performers-in-the-round
provide and project not only characterization but a sense of the envi-
ronment that contains them. For its part, the encircling audience con-
tributes its collective visual imagination to setting the scene as well as
providing the physical boundary for the action and serving both as mir-
ror and sounding board for the performers.

In addition to the augmented basic actor illumination
necessitated by complete audience encirclement, there is an
equally heavy demand placed on atmospheric lighting. Since
the central form permits only a minimum of dimensional
scenic embellishment, an artful arrangement of projections and
other special effect illumination is essential in order to establish mood and location. Also, since equal intensity is required
on all sides in order to accommodate the vision requirements
for an encircling audience, the problem of depth and model-
ing, readily achieved on proscenium frame stages by balancing
light and shadow, here becomes a challenge requiring the highest levels of technical competence.

Also, the intense actor lighting tends to spill onto the faces
and fluttering programs of a surrounding audience. In addition, the performance space, ringed by an audience, presents
some portion of this audience as background to any position
along the periphery. While some audience members might enjoy
looking at their fellow spectators, others find it distracting. With
actors facing in various directions, vocal projection may also be

a problem. If an actor tells a joke facing one portion of the audience and that portion laughs, the rest of the audience may wonder what was so funny.

Because of all these technical considerations plus the overwhelming demands of creating and maintaining that special quality of heightened reality which is at the heart of the theatrical experience, the central staging form, while deceptively simple to set up, is often difficult to handle. It seems to work best for such nonverbal presentations as circuses and ice shows. Seasonal music tents presenting revivals of familiar Broadway musicals, with body-mikes reinforcing multidirectioned voices, often succeed in entertaining large, relatively undemanding audiences.

On a less professional level, when central staging is used as a variety of instant theatre, its informality and simplicity may be disarmingly effective, particularly when performers are unskilled and effects are generalized. Here, a lack of art reflected in the faces of a tolerant audience may succeed in creating a form of magic probably very close to the experience of primitive ritual.

The impression persists that central focus or arena staging is extremely simple to achieve and therefore desirable. But working with or on it quickly demonstrates how difficult are the obstacles to be overcome. It is a major challenge to the set designers who cannot get the convincing effects they are used to, to the lighting designers faced with having to light actors facing in many directions who have to be seen by audiences viewing from every point, to directors who need to be sure every member of the surrounding audience sees and hears equally, to the actors who try to perform knowing at all times half of the audience is experiencing only their backs, and to the audience members who may feel cheated when an actor's big scene is delivered to the other side of the hall.

In a highly evolved theatre where expectations of artistic achievement run high, anything but a complete mastery of the central form will frequently disappoint, for it takes a high degree of skill to get an encirclement of individual spectators to react to the essence of a theatrical event as a unit. The effectiveness of any live theatrical event is dependant on the degree to which an audience is capable of reacting to given stimuli in a unified manner. The impact of a performance, therefore, must be as equal as possible for every spectator, and when, for any reason whatsoever, this is not possible, then the form of the presentation must be rethought. The paradox of its being a form simultaneously primitive and sophisticated presents unusual challenges to anyone attempting to present fully-realized theatrical events in terms of central-focus staging.

> *Although essential to theatre-in-the-round, the element of focus should play a significant role in the development of all forms of theatre — thereby facilitating audience concentration on the event and encouraging actors to capitalize on such concentration for the effectiveness of their performances.*

FOUR

Platform

A prominent platform, originally conceived as an adjunct to a performance circle in antiquity, has been an essential feature of all workable theatres since the Middle Ages.

The provision of a clearly marked-off area reserved for the sole use of performers is an essential component of any evolved theatre form. As a base for a theatrical event, it can enhance the effectiveness of performance by reinforcing an audience's ability to concentrate on the creative intention.

The surface on which a performance is mounted — the base, the platform, the pedestal — is where the performers play out the moment-to-moment rhythms of the event. A performer, moving from position to position according to some preconceived plan — upstage, downstage, stage right, stage left — embodies the dramatic intention and gives shape to the performance.

When this surface is raised above the level of an audience and is backed by a partition serving to conceal dressing rooms and other offstage functions as well as providing a background for the action, a greater degree of concentration than is ordinarily afforded by the purely central form is achieved both for performers and spectators.

With seating removed from anywhere between one-third to one-half of the circle surrounding the performance area, the audience, except for those on the extreme sides, is able to concentrate on the performance without the confusion of having to view it against a background of other members of the audience.

In addition, as a specifically designated pedestal for performance, the platform can provide a stage director with far greater control over subtlety and nuance. Production lighting, freed from the necessity of having to accommodate a totally encircling audience, can usually deliver its intended effects with far fewer instruments. For their part, the performers, liberated by not having to project their assumed personas expressively to an audience surrounding them on all four sides, can more readily grasp the totality of an assembled audience and be capable of directing their energies with greater economy of effort.

· · ·

Although the raised stage originated in the amphitheaters of the ancient world to complement and eventually to usurp the ritualistic performance circle, it was not until the Middle Ages that the platform really came into its own. Compact and portable, it provided a convenient solution for itinerant performers who could set themselves up at a crossroads or in a marketplace and display their talents whenever and wherever the opportunity presented itself. By this simple theatrical method they were able to keep alive the rudiments of an evolving performance tradition during a period of cultural chaos which precluded the establishment of fixed theatres.

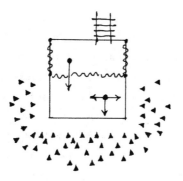

A portable platform, elevated structurally and therefore independent of the particular condition of pavement or earth on which it happened to be placed, provided wandering players with a familiar and consistent surface on which to play out a previously rehearsed event. A curtained-off back area could conceal any offstage preparation and the curtain itself could act as a neutralizing plane and entranceway onto the main field of action.

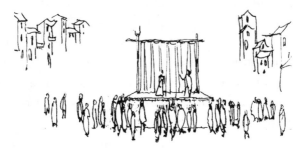

Performers emerging through this curtain could confront and engage the attention of an audience gathered on three sides of the platform. Relieved of the burden of having to relate to a totally encircling audience, they could more readily direct their performances front and center and from side to side, rarely having to turn their backs on any segment of their public.

Evidence indicates that the typical platform of the Middle Ages was a simple trestle-stage backed by a curtain attached to a wooden frame. The platform was unfurnished except perhaps for a stool or two if the action required it. Performers made their way forward onto the platform from behind the concealing curtain or peered over the top of the backing to simulate looking down from a battlement or from the upper story of a house.

It was very much a popular form of theatre, depending for its effect on an intimate actor/audience relationship. Basic and forthright, it presented a neutral location for the passions or poetry inherent in the situations typically being dramatized. Because its backing served more to conceal offstage actors than to provide a background image for the performance, it encouraged spectators to contribute their creative imaginations to visualizing the atmosphere of the event.

Later, when the portable platform was introduced into the confines of an urban courtyard, two major developments occurred. One was that the audience was provided with a variety of places from which to view the performance. Not only were the spectators able to mass themselves in front and to the sides of the platform erected on the floor of the courtyard, they could also position themselves at the windows and balconies of the surrounding buildings. If the courtyard happened to be that of an inn, the exterior passageways which ran along the sides of the building on all floor levels could be provided with seating and these locations could be sold on a reserved basis.

Installed temporarily within an inn-yard, the platform stage — still open to the sky — began to integrate itself into a multilevel audience arrangement facilitated by the pre-existing enclosure. This improvised actor/audience relationship foreshadowed future architectural solutions.

The other major development was that the performance staged within the enclosure of the surrounding buildings was effectively removed from the bustle of the urban scene. Such isolation from outside distraction produced the possibility for a degree of concentration and control of theatrical effect otherwise unattainable.

• • •

In England, the tradition of strolling players setting up their portable platforms within the confines of the inn-yard led to further important developments. This arrangement, with spectators sitting or standing on ground level before and to the sides of the platform and around the open passageways of the surrounding building, evolved into the self-contained popular theatre structure we associate with the playhouses which originally produced the plays of Shakespeare. Here, the platform, thrust out into the midst of the spectators and surrounded by tiers of galleries, provided a type of playhouse well suited to virtuoso acting. Built of wood, it presented an architectural setting which was both so neutral and so evocative that it made specific scenic effects unnecessary.

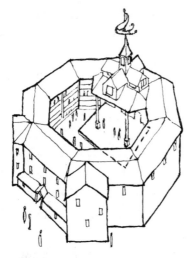

From the installation of portable platforms within the multilevel enclosures of inn-yards evolved the model for a free-standing structure specifically designed for theatrical presentation: the open-to-the-sky, Elizabethan playhouse (shown here, the Globe) with its prominent platform and integrated auditorium.

Such a theatre, a place with its own architectural integrity and yet completely adaptable, was the perfect setting for the kind of drama that encouraged the spoken word to evoke the poetic image. In such a theatre, rapid changes of scene were readily accomplished by verbal stimulation of the audience's imagination. Detailed stage decoration was of minor importance and yet the total effect of the theatrical event, occurring on a clearly marked platform within an intimately scaled auditorium, must have been extraordinarily spirited and convincing.

In the Elizabethan popular theatre, the stage itself was a wooden platform approximately forty feet square jutting out into the very center of the pit. At the rear of the platform were doors which opened to reveal interiors and above these, on a second level, were galleries to suggest an upper inner stage. The half roof over the platform, supported by two pillars set midway on the sides of the stage floor, contained a trapdoor through which performers and set pieces could be raised and lowered.

The physical arrangement of the platform allowed performance patterns far more varied and dynamic than otherwise possible. The fact that the main playing area was a square rather than a shallow rectangle permitted the actors to move from side to side and front to rear with equal effectiveness. This increased the potential for depth in stage groupings and expanded the possibilities for a more dynamic mise-en-scène. Entrances could be made from the doorways in the backing or even from the pit. The upper stage permitted vertical staging and traps in the stage floor allowed for fast disappearances and appearances from below.

The London Globe of Shakespeare's time was a large theatre capable of accommodating thousands within its wooden "O," yet the "O" was so devised as to bring even the most remote gallery spectators close enough into the world of the performance so that a rare degree of intimacy was achieved. Because front and center stage and the center of the house were practically identical, the closest possible contact between performers and audience could be achieved and maintained. An actor standing downstage center could rivet and hold the attention of a vast audience standing on the ground and arranged in the galleries. The flexibility and neutrality of the platform encouraged virtuosity in performance and, because of the design of the playhouse, a high degree of audience focus and contact was sustained.

• • •

Just as the introduction of the portable platform into the inn-yards provided the model for the evolving popular theatre of Shakespeare, so the introduction of the platform stage into the ballrooms of the ducal courts started the process which developed into the highly sophisticated form of the baroque theatre.

At the Italian courts, the platform typically was set up at the narrow end of a ballroom with broad flights of steps leading down to the dance floor. Since the dance floor was the principal performance area, the observers grouped themselves along the edges of the room in a U-shaped arrangement. The platform at one end of the space was considered to be an accessory to the performance and served mainly as a base for accompanying scenic illusion.

When demountable platforms were set up in the palatial interiors of the ducal courts, the platform was used not primarily for performance but for ancillary scenic effects. The performance took place on the ballroom floor with the spectators — depending on their rank — either sitting or standing around it with their attention divided between observing actors performing on their level and scenic effects taking place at the end of the room on a raised platform.

Special effects and transformations, calculated to tease and delight the eye, were liberally employed to complement the floor-bound action. Occasionally, set pieces on wheels, similar to medieval pageant wagons, were drawn onto the floor to add to the fanciful effects emanating from the raised stage. In this way, the temporary scenic embellishments designed for the performance could fuse atmospherically with the already-existing ornate interiors into which they were introduced. Thus was established the opulent style which informed the evolution of both stage and auditorium in the court theatres of the 17th and 18th centuries.

. . .

Throughout Europe in the 17th century, a contest of sorts was being waged between advocates of the unadorned platform stage favored by the English and advocates of the new scenic techniques being developed at a rapid rate by the Italians. In England, the tradition of the platform stage as it had evolved in the Elizabethan public playhouses was far too firmly entrenched to allow the novelty of scenic illusion to gain much of a foothold. The actors preferred to dominate the forward edge of the platform, thereby capturing the attention of the audience with their words and emotions rather than allowing themselves to be drawn into and absorbed within the kind of elaborate pictorial representation which might threaten their supremacy.

Eventually the English theatre did evolve into a theatre of illusion. But the tradition of the platform remained strong in the form of a prominent forestage jutting out into the auditorium with side doors for performer access.

The development of the platform as the principal base for indoor per-formance resulted in the dominant forestage — the English response to steady encroachments of scenic illusion emanating from the continent.

Toward the end of the 17th century, however, the manag-er of London's Drury Lane, seeking to increase the audience capacity in the pit, took it upon himself to remove the for-ward portion of the forestage altogether. He also converted the no longer needed downstage actors' entrance doors into additional boxes for the audience. The actors resisted by insisting that a significant portion of the upstage space be dedicated to the construction of two additional entrance doors to take the place of those which had been transformed into boxes. The tradition of the Elizabethan platform remained exceedingly strong, and the actors fought hard not to yield their dominant position by receding into what was fast becoming the picture-frame stage.

· · ·

There is a profound difference between the effect of a performance given on a highly visible and accessible platform in close contact with an actively engaged audience and the effect of a performance given within a pictorial surround which vies with the actors and envelops them in its atmosphere. The former places great emphasis on the ability of performers to create their world in terms of action and expression; the latter depends on scenic illusion to complement the performers as they inhabit a controlled scenic environment which an audience does not physically share.

The question of which approach better serves the theatrical event has been a subject of lively debate since the middle of the 17th century. As will be seen, in the 18th, 19th, and 20th centuries the framed stage came to dominate mainstream theatre architecture. But in reaction to this, a number of exposed platforms — especially the thrust stages built in Canada and the United States since World War II — were conceived in order to present alternatives to the status quo.

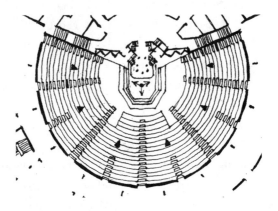

The concept of the prominent forestage was resuscitated in the flurry of experimental theatre construction in the decades following World War II, most notably, as shown here, with the 1957 Festival Theatre in Stratford, Ontario.

The development of the thrust stage backed by a unit set and flanked by audience on three sides effected the release of the performer from what was perceived as the clutches of an all-encompassing scenic illusion.

Our contemporary theatres which choose to hearken back to the qualities of the platform stage usually feature prominent thrust stages surrounded on three sides by audience and backed either by some variation on the all-purpose multilevel scaffold of the Elizabethan theatre or a framed enclosure capable of accommodating changeable scenery. The general impression that one gets upon entering such an environment is that the forestage and its overhead lighting dominate and that the scenic backing — no matter how elaborate — is somehow incidental.

Depending on where one is seated, the backing either complements the platform or remains outside the focus of the action. From front and center positions within the auditorium, the actors are seen against the backing and seem to be performing within the scenic investiture much as they would if they were on an arched or end stage. From positions on either side, however, the actors appear released from the environment of the backing and are typically observed performing against the opposite section of the audience. From these locations, the spectators must shift their gaze from the action to the setting in order to be able to integrate the effect of the intended production design.

In the thrust form, audience position relative to the platform varies and the impact of the production on the spectator varies, too. If scenic backing is crucial to the event, the thrust form can diminish the effectiveness of a performance. If, however, the atmospheric contribution of the set is of minor consequence and the action on the thrust is the point of the staging, then the relative intimacy of the form can yield measurable satisfaction.

Unfortunately, in many examples of such theatres, directors have to struggle with the problem of relating the action not only to the setting but to a three-sided audience that is not necessarily responding as a unit to the moment-to-moment pacing of the performance. Audience reaction is often fragmented and it is not uncommon for some members of the audience to be better served than others. The results can often be disheartening for actors, and many — after experiencing the often severe challenges of performing in a thrust theatre where, stepping far downstage into the center of the house, they seem to be leaving much of the audience behind them — tend to prefer the relative control of the more conventional framed stage.

However, the experiments that the director Tyrone Guthrie undertook with thrust stages in Edinburgh before World War II and later in Stratford, Ontario, exerted a strong influence in the United States especially in regional and academic applications. A combination of the Elizabethan platform with the fan-shaped Greco-Roman auditorium proved tempting to many of those intent on liberating performers from the perceived constraints of what had become the conventional proscenium frame theatre.

In sum, with the thrust stage, the actor, released from the frame, can attain a degree of intimacy and immediacy which can have a direct impact on an audience. On the other hand, the thrust means that members of the audience to the sides of the thrust are often left frustrated, resulting in a fragmentation of performance effect. In platform theatre designs of the past half century, the shape of the thrust and the shape of the corresponding auditorium have been modified again and again in attempts to achieve the best possible effect in an infinitely variable balancing act. Sometimes these experiments have succeeded — sometimes not — but all of them contribute insights into the persistent problem of how to relate relatively large audiences to stage performances in an optimal way.

FIVE

Frame

A frame to incorporate or conceal production equipment as well as to define the atmospheric extent of a performance is the mark of any technologically advanced theatre.

Sometimes the presentation of a theatrical event calls for more than a designated acting area set before an audience. What is then needed is a device which can both define the environment for the performance and incorporate the technical apparatus necessary for the required scenic embellishment. What hitherto may have seemed a fairly straightforward actor/audience relationship may suddenly acquire complexity as more control over illusions and effects occurring on the stage is desired.

The attempt to accommodate these greater technical demands can have considerable impact on performers and audiences alike. From the audience's perspective, there may be wings or set pieces defining the vertical edges of the stage picture or conspicuous banks of lights hovering over the acting area.

As the performers face their audiences, they must relate to them through an encompassing frame of technical apparatus that often distances them from the auditorium and sets up an impression of isolation.

The zone that is created — like a two-way portal defining a reality for each separate sphere — serves to divide as well as unite one world and the other. On the one hand, the frame provides the means for enhancing the light and sound needed to complement the work of the performers; on the other, it defines and isolates the environment of the event for those witnessing it. The complexities involved in satisfying these two functions can be staggering and often counterproductive to the smooth functioning of the event, impeding the crucial interchange that is at the core of a successful actor/audience relationship.

The paradox of the frame as facilitator of stage illusion and as impediment to direct communication has haunted theorists since the middle of the 17th century. Concerted attempts to liberate performers from the grip of scenic illusion have lately brought the relevancy of the framed stage into serious question. Nevertheless, the form most commonly in use today persists in being the solidly framed stage. As the standard for theatres built around the world, this self-contained volume with fly space above and wings on either side is meant to accommodate the production of just about any form of live entertainment — and generally succeeds in doing so to a remarkable degree.

Typically, as the house lights dim and a blush of light appears on a vast expanse of velour, an audience experiences a sense of anticipation for what lies beyond. The curtain rises, and the effect of whatever is revealed depends not only on the characteristics of the particular production installed there but also on our ability — enhanced or diminished by the quality of the auditorium which contains us — to receive and react to it.

Even in this electronic age, the considerable attraction the framed stage continues to exert on the collective imagination is directly attributable to its ability to conjure up, without revealing its means, evocative environments in the service of a dramatic situation. As a self-contained volume of space, it provides, with its framing arch, its overhead flies, and its neutral void awaiting the design wizardry and performance skills of any particular production, an efficient and workable system for the presentation of most theatrical events.

• • •

The pictorial stage as we know it has had a long history of development going back to Renaissance Italy where court festivities encouraged the creation of elaborate decorative effects. As these displays were eventually put to theatrical use, they were installed behind frames not only to contain their compositions but also to mask the machinery that made their wide-ranging and often astonishing effects possible.

Indeed, some of the earliest prototypes of the framed stage served more to accommodate illusions than to provide locations for performance. The Teatro Farnese, built in Parma in the early 17th century, featured a framed enclosure devoted to scenic display recessed into the end wall of a ballroom, while the players, as was their custom, continued to perform at the center of the ballroom floor. The spectators, for their part, directed their attention toward the performers while seated in a semi-encircling U-shaped arrangement of tiered seating. Only when the performance dictated did they divert their gaze to the effects taking place at the far end of the room behind the frame.

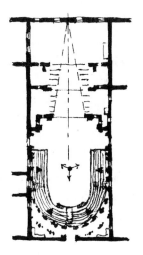

In the Farnese Palace, the temporary platform as a base for scenic illusion evolved into a permanent feature framed by an arch and incorporated into a narrow end wall of a ballroom. Beyond the arch, a raked stage rigged for changeable wings, borders, and drops extended back to a depth almost equal to the dimension of the ballroom itself.

Although, in the case of the Teatro Farnese, the principal action was still confined to the ballroom floor, the development of the curtained stage of illusion exerted a considerable impact of its own. As a device originally intended for the presentation of pictorial illusions incidental to performance, the framed stage began more and more to lure the principal action of the event away from the auditorium space and into the confines of its all-encompassing scenic environment.

As theatrical presentations became more formal — more scripted and less of a floor show — the focus of performance began to shift from the ballroom floor to the enclosure beyond the arch with its ever more elaborate and encompassing scenic resources. In order to facilitate this adjustment, audience seating shifted as well. The tiered U-shaped structure at the periphery of the dance floor still accommodated a goodly number of spectators. However, the floor itself, no longer devoted to performance, was given over to rows of chairs facing the framed stage, permitting more of the audience better views into the marked-off world of scenic illusion.

. . .

Several generations of painters and draughtsmen, experimenting with linear perspective, had successfully demonstrated that illusions of depth were readily achievable on flat surfaces. This discovery revolutionized scenic design by providing a workable method for achieving effects of unlimited space on two-dimensional planes. Its influence on the subsequent arrangement of stages was profound.

Consequently, the volume of the stage was subdivided by a series of regularly spaced planes parallel to the framed opening. These continued all the way to the back wall where the vanishing point was established. Around this vanishing point all aspects of the setting could be organized in direct relationship to one point of view — a point of view firmly fixed within the ducal box.

At each of the lateral positions, just beyond the audience's line of sight, was located the machinery for supporting or suspending scenic elements. From below the stage floor, from the wing spaces to the sides and from the fly space above, the coordination of the various devices could effect simultaneous shifts of wings, borders, and drops resulting in instantaneous set changes.

The illusion of depth achieved by depicting elements in diminishing size on successive wings and borders framing the stage space and organizing them according to the rules of linear perspective was truly impressive. Lateral wings depicting fore-shortened series of columns and overhead borders represent-ing ceiling beams evoked a convincing illusion of interior space. Lateral wings in the form of trees with sky borders above suggested outdoor locations. Combined with pictorial back-cloths which completed the composition around the estab-lished vanishing point, these framing elements created a ser-viceable version of deep space. The floor, which sloped upward from the proscenium line toward the vanishing point, rein-forced this illusion of depth.

This system of stage decoration accommodated a complete range of scenic possibilities. As adaptable as it was compre-hensive, it outlasted its aristocratic origins and went on to influence the course of the popular theatre well into the 19th century. Even today, a system of wings, borders, and drops continues in force especially in productions requiring lateral exits and entrances for large numbers of performers as in bal-let, opera, and musical theatre.

· · ·

Interestingly enough, most of the features of the framed stage as we now know it had been invented by the middle of the 17th century. The house curtain, which filled the entire prosce-nium opening, gave scene designers the opportunity to reveal and conceal their changeable pictorial arrangements with dramatic suddenness. Often, however, it was hard to resist the temptation to keep the curtain up during scene changes, allowing transformations from one setting to the next to occur in full sight of a predictably bedazzled audience.

As these developments were taking place in the stage area, complementary modifications were being made in the auditorium area as well. The U-shaped seating sections of the early ballroom theatres were expanded vertically on a number of levels, frequently reaching to the height of the proscenium arch in order to accommodate an ever-increasing audience capacity.

In time, the U-shaped galleries, now physically joined to the proscenium arch, began to bulge laterally until they assumed a form that resembled a horseshoe, thereby maximizing audience capacity while creating a sense of containment for the auditorium.

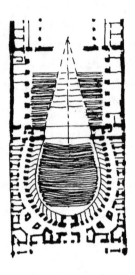

Typically, the ducal box, centrally located on the first tier opposite the stage, had optimal views into the scenic perspective, whereas the boxes incorporated into the proscenium arch to the sides of the orchestra pit had the most distorted views. In between, the individual boxes and galleries shared the pleasures of the stage in varying degrees according to their specific locations. Meanwhile the floor, outfitted with benches or chairs and sloped to accommodate vertical sightlines, provided some of the more advantageous — though less prestigious — locations in the house.

Now that actors had been absorbed into the scenic world beyond the arch, performances became more and more illusionistic in style and contemporary dramatic literature tended to exploit this. Since just about any environment imaginable could be conjured up for theatrical purposes and sets could be changed instantaneously, plays were written with multiple scenes occurring in many different locations, taking full advantage of this capability. Subject matter ranged from the mythic and the legendary to the outright fantastical and the creative teams responsible for producing these entertainments stressed scenic illusion above all else.

The audience was treated to ascending and descending clouds bearing gods, goddesses, and heavenly choirs, to stormy seas with miniature vessels being tossed about between animated waves, to buildings composed of flats hinged to collapse on cue and to terrifyingly lifelike conflagrations. Candles or lamps placed between the setting planes and masked by overhead borders and lateral wings illuminated the scenery while color media — red and blue liquid in bottles placed in front of these light sources — added mood and atmosphere. Footlights, masked from the audience by reflector shields, lit the performers' faces and a repertory of sound effects reinforced the intended illusions.

These scenic effects were very persuasive, especially when viewed from the ducal box at the rear of the auditorium one floor level above the pit. Of course, the lesser locations above and below and to the sides, reflecting descending scales of rank, had less satisfactory views, but the general impact of this pictorial illusion was nonetheless captivating.

To accommodate these scenic developments, the platform began to extend ever farther back from the arch until the stage became as deep as or deeper than the auditorium. Because rapid shifts of wings required additional space on the sides, the stage house also broadened, often to twice the width of the proscenium opening. Drops and set pieces let down from and hoisted up to above the line of audience vision required a height above the platform often in excess of two and one-half times the height of the proscenium arch itself. A considerable space below the platform was also required for the tracks and carriages which moved the wings laterally and for the hoists that permitted vertical movement of set pieces and performers through the floor traps. All of this resulted in a stage house volume which often loomed larger than the auditorium itself.

• • •

Just as these production devices were reaching their apogee in the court theatres on the continent, the English designer Inigo Jones toured Italy for the purpose of observing this new stagecraft. He was impressed by the resources of the curtained stage and by the power of the changeable settings to enrapture an audience. On his return to England he set about creating his own versions of the settings-in-depth, incorporating innovative techniques of pictorial illusion in a series of designs for court masques.

Although these experiments were warmly appreciated by their aristocratic audiences and contributed much to the evolution of English theatre building after the Restoration of 1660, the popular English obsession with the platform — nourished in large part by still-fresh recollections of the more presentational techniques of the Shakespearean theatre — provided a stubbornly persistent opposition to a complete acceptance of the theatre of illusion. As a result of such conflicting attitudes, there developed a hybrid frame-with-forestage form which set the course for theatre architecture in England and America throughout the following one hundred and fifty years.

The relationship of an acting platform to scenic illusion always has a direct influence on the arrangement of audience positions within any auditorium. As we saw in the continental theatres, when the stage space was restricted to the area behind the arch the sightlines proved most satisfactory for the ducal box and a good deal less so for the rest of the audience. In the more democratic English examples, however, where the forestage platform remained the principal place for performance, the sight lines of the multilevelled U-shaped house related more directly to the projecting platform and less to the scenic display receding in depth behind the arch.

In the continental examples, the U-shaped tiers of boxes lining the auditorium from pit to dome created a festive atmosphere for the event but did not provide an efficient arrangement of positions from which the majority of spectators could partake equally of the visual splendors unfolding on stage. To make matters worse, the box fronts defining the audience space, at first laid out on an oval plan, were later, to permit increased capacity, bowed out like a horseshoe with the ends merging at an angle with the frame defining the stage opening. In such arrangements, views from the flanking boxes into the stage space proved difficult and became almost impossible the closer one got to the proscenium arch. From these extreme positions it was far easier to observe activities in the auditorium and within the ducal box than to see what was transpiring on stage.

As the playhouses spread beyond the courts and into the municipalities, the central box was invariably preserved for the occasional use of visiting dignitaries. With the rise of the middle classes in the early 19th century, its flanking boxes, now available by subscription, became equally elaborate and capacious. As a parlor away from home, they served as much for conversation, social intercourse, and intrigue as for watching a performance. As it was often considered to be of greater importance to be observed in one's box than to attend on a particular performance, this attitude had a marked effect on the type of entertainment offered.

So socially ingrained was the box system that, even when, in the course of the 19th century, individual boxes were being replaced by rows of chairs unbroken by dividing walls, the tiers still preserved their distinctive horseshoe plan — and this remained so even though sight lines from the sides were still very often inadequate for viewing whatever was taking place beyond the arch.

· · ·

Generally speaking, wherever the theatre of scenic illusion flourished, the plays written for it tended to favor spectacle over subtle character development. A liberal accompaniment of music and dance caused drama to be more sung and mimed than acted, and exaggerated gestures and the broader effects of production encouraged theatres to be built at the scale of opera houses. In fact, by the beginning of the 19th century, the type of theatre developed for Italian opera — a framed stage accompanied by many tiers of galleries — had become the accepted ideal for nearly all theatre architecture.

Taking advantage of the experiments in form and production that had evolved under royal patronage during the Baroque period, commercial opera entrepreneurs joined forces with speculative builders and municipal officials to create greatly enlarged versions of the court theatres. These were built to attract the widest possible segments of a newly entitled public to the sort of entertainment hitherto available only to the nobility. As a result, the fully developed framed stage theatre — characterized by the high, wide, and deep stagehouse and the oval or horseshoe-shaped auditorium of many levels served by an elaborate system of circulation areas and monumental foyers — achieved a dominant position within the cultural fabric of every major city in the Western World. And this form of theatre was used not only for opera, but for all types of theatrical presentations.

• • •

The first real reaction against this traditional opera-type theatre occurred, oddly enough, in conjunction with the production of opera. In the 1870s Richard Wagner, eager to provide an environment for his operas that would concentrate all of an audience's attention on his work, developed a radically new approach to auditorium design. Retaining all of the resources of the pictorial stage, he rejected the horseshoe form along with its many distractions in favor of an arrangement that would guarantee unobstructed sight lines and a satisfactory point of view for every member of the audience.

In a theatre built according to his own aesthetic specifications, Wagner insured the primacy of his operatic productions over the structure that would contain them. All audience attention was to be directed toward the theatrical presentation and nothing else.

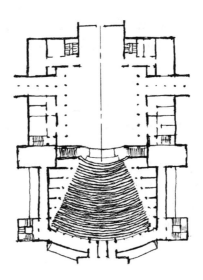

While totally accepting the deep stage of scenic illusion complete with the techniques and machinery developed by the Italians, he nevertheless rejected the form of their auditorium with its social and hierarchical distractions. Gone were the lateral tiers of boxes and galleries and an orchestra pit that exposed the musicians to view. Instead he established a sloped fan-shaped auditorium arrangement that focussed the atten-tion of every spectator onto the stage picture.

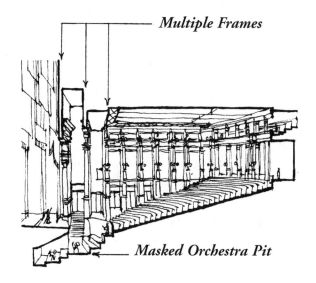

Multiple Frames

Masked Orchestra Pit

As viewed through a succession of frames diminishing in size over an orchestra pit built partially beneath the stage and totally obscured from the audience by a curved shield, the stage picture seemed to defy the limitations of ordinary space and to hover as if emerging from beyond a "magic gulf."

In the Festspielhaus at Bayreuth, the main body of the audience faced the stage on one level arranged in concentrically curved rows sloping down toward the stage. As a concession to convention and to accommodate necessary royal patronage, a single gallery was placed across the rear wall above and behind the general audience area. But no longer was everything on stage presented primarily for the royal pleasure.

Without wraparound tiers of boxes and galleries, the Bayreuth auditorium represented the essence of an egalitarian arrangement. Unfortunately, however, such an approach reduced the capacity of the auditorium to well below the economic levels necessary for mounting commercial operatic production and, as a result, it had little direct effect on other, less subsidized, opera buildings. It did, however, have a considerable influence on the auditorium arrangement of nonoperatic theatres which were being built toward the end of the 19th century, especially when advances in cantilever design permitted the addition of broad, deep balconies without the need for supporting columns. These extended the capacity of the house on several levels, one above the other, facing toward the stage picture.

In the 20th century, this same general form — forward-facing rows of seats focussed on the performance area with sloping balconies above — provided the model for the development of the motion picture theatre which required a similar unobstructed point of view to a projection screen for all members of an audience.

So, in terms of audience handling, Wagner's theatre marked the beginning of a revolt against the autocratic Italian form. It introduced democracy into theatre design by establishing a shared point of view for an entire audience into the scenic world beyond the arch.

The Bayreuth theatre was also significant in that it took advantage of evolving techniques in controlled lighting. For the first time, with the development of both gas and electricity, it was possible to control auditorium as well as stage lighting.

Until then, if the auditorium were to be darkened, the chandeliers suspended over the spectators had to be raised up out of sight through traps in the ceiling. However, the lamps on the fixed wall sconces could not be as readily extinguished. Therefore, the spectators were often as visible to one another during a performance as the performers themselves.

Now, with the development of modern lighting techniques, it was possible to plunge an auditorium into darkness at the beginning of a performance, to release an audience from the awareness of its peers, and to concentrate all light, and therefore all attention, on the performance space.

The experience of attending a performance in so controlled an environment was seductive. The actors and the settings that they inhabited appeared to be larger-than-life, less like us and the world as we know it. Such an impression of otherworldliness — so supportive of the Wagnerian oeuvre — proved frequently frustrating under less heightened circumstances, frustrating enough, in fact, to trigger rebellion against the distancing effect of the arch.

· · ·

With the introduction of a more humanly scaled approach to drama in the last quarter of the 19th century came a desire to establish more intimate — less segregated — relationships between performers and audience. The de-emphasis of spectacle in favor of subtler renderings of character created a need for smaller, less ornamented, more unified theatrical spaces.

Ironically, at the same time as this tendency toward greater intimacy was gaining its adherents, the convention of separating stage and auditorium — until then an aesthetic solution to masking the mechanics of the backstage from the audience — was being reinforced by the application of new, stricter fire regulations in places of public assembly. After a series of disastrous fires, the provision of a fire-resistant curtain in a solidly built wall isolating stage from auditorium became mandatory in most large cities. In ensuing years, however, with the development of more fire-resistant building methods and materials, these regulations were somewhat relaxed permitting other forms of theatres to be built consistent with fire codes and without having to rely on the fixed arch and fire curtain as the sole method of fire containment.

As far as production was concerned, the more naturalistic dramas of the late 19th century, dependent as they were on subtler nuances of performance, seemed ill-at-ease within the parallel flat planes of wings, borders, and backdrops that until then were the norm for the framed stage. The more intimate and probing psychology of the new dramas of Ibsen and Chekhov, for example, demanded greater degrees of spatial containment than the conventional method provided. As a result, the separated lateral wings were transformed into continuous side walls which ran obliquely back from the arch to form a contained wedge of space with a closure to the rear.

The "new naturalism" encouraged the abandonment of conventional wings, borders, and backdrops in favor of solidly built, three-sided, ceilinged enclosures. Performers were integrated into an all-encompassing "slice-of-life" observed through a defining arch.

Entrances into the performance space now had to be made through doors realistically built into the three walls forming the typical scenic interior and glimpses into the world beyond were provided through windows backed by atmospheric flats or drops. When, in due course, ceiling pieces rather than borders were brought down to join the tops of the three surrounding walls, the interior volume of what became known as the box set was complete and a spatial environment suitable for a more naturalistic form of drama was achieved.

However, when the production required an exterior setting and limitations of space precluded the installation of a cyclorama, wings and borders had to be reintroduced, if only to mask the offstage areas from audience view. In order to counteract the apparent artificiality of this vestigial convention, three dimensional set pieces were often installed within this flat environment to give at least an impression of the new naturalism.

By the beginning of the First World War the novelty of reproducing naturalistic, slice-of-life environments on a stage in terms of three-dimensional, spatially contained, pictorially accurate scenery had worn thin. Theatre artists, the public, and the critics began to yearn for the more heightened experience that a less literal, perhaps more evocative, form of theatre could offer.

· · ·

The picture-frame stage, with or without forestage or apron, has been the predominant theatre form for the last century and a half. It gained this status because of what seemed its considerable advantage over earlier forms. Its acceptability is based on its capacity to control illusion and to hide the mechanics by which it makes its effects.

Furthermore, a generally accepted standard of stage size and built-in technical support allows touring companies to arrive, install their production elements within the empty box, and depart to the next empty box taking their production with them. In theatres where production follows production with no continuity of creative personnel, the picture-frame stage presents a tabula rasa and the opportunity for that empty space to be filled in countless ways.

So the picture-frame stage is the form of choice for most commercial houses worldwide. However, while the picture-frame stage provides production control, it also creates a sense of separation from its intended audience, which feels it is observing the theatrical event through an invisible fourth wall. While some consider this to be an advantage, others feel it to be a disadvantage. Actors sometimes feel removed from their audiences. Directors can feel frustrated, wanting to make their productions "connect" more forcefully. To some, the distancing of theatrical presentations behind the frame can begin to feel unreal and elitist.

Since the early decades of this century, along with the growing preponderance of picture-frame stages came a strong urge to "break the frame," to return to earlier less rigid arrangements and to develop new forms in the design of theatres. After World War I, opportunities arose for renewed experimentation in substance and form, an experimentation which continues to this day.

SIX

Experimentation
...Adjustment

If most of 19th century theatre, awash in scenic illusion and
lingering traces of the baroque tradition, seemed typically larger-
than-life, developments in playwrighting from the 1880s
onward favored dramatizations lived at a more lifelike scale.
Consequently, the majority of theatres with their cavernous
spaces and aristocratic trappings began to seem too large, too
sumptuous, too irrelevant to be able to accommodate this new
approach.

Unfortunately, greater degrees of nuance in performance
and the theatre structures which could support more intimate
actor/audience relationships did not readily jibe with the economic realities of the commercial theatre at the turn of the

20th century. Considering relative values of land and construction, taxation and earning potential, there were limits to just how small a capacity theatre a developer might be willing to build. A goodly number of nonmusical houses were in fact built around the turn of the century but they were rarely as intimate as innovative directors would have preferred.

The fully evolved framed stage, efficient and universally adopted and therefore capable of accommodating any kind of touring production, seemed a relatively safe investment. Consequently, this type of theatre was built in cities and towns from coast-to-coast and around the world. Innovators were forced to look elsewhere to find the kinds of environments that might satisfy their aesthetic needs.

• • •

As a reaction to immense amounts of technological sophistication contained within a stubbornly baroque package, a yearning for simpler, more direct presentation began to take hold. It was recalled that the cause of dramatic literature was better served when actors and audiences could confront one another more directly and stage conventions eliminated the need for elaborate scenic illusion.

Experimental groups working in the early 20th century soon found that conventional playhouses could not begin to accommodate the degree of freedom they had in mind. Instead, they sought out nontraditional, nontheatrical, structures. Warehouses, lofts, and factories, especially those with few interior columns, along with the occasional abandoned church or lecture hall, were seized upon and adapted for theatrical use.

A particular ideal of the new style of theatre was to merge actors with spectators within a common spatial envelope, but this created a new set of performance conditions that had to be confronted and solved. No longer would the glare of onstage lighting be discreetly shielded from an audience by an intervening arch. Instead, these practitioners declared that frank disclosure of technical support systems might aid in creating more theatrical, less naturalistic environments, and that performance innovations of all sorts would be a direct result.

Meanwhile, contemporary developments in painting and sculpture discouraged any mere photographic reproduction of nature. In particular, the abstract and nonobjective movements began to influence theatrical production in ways that made it seem irrelevant even to consider attempting to replicate nature on the stage either in terms of decoration or performance. Techniques for fooling the eye soon yielded to increased concern for stimulating the mind.

The experiments of such visionaries as Gordon Craig and Adolph Appia demonstrated that the environment devised for any particular performance could express a psychological, rather than a merely dimensional, reality. As a result, the box set, along with the slice of life that it denoted, was devalued and deliberate attempts were made to find atmospheric equivalents in terms of selective representation or evocative symbols.

The first quarter of the 20th century was also marked by efforts to develop specialized theatre types that might relate more directly to the actual demands of dramatic presentation.

Theatrical environments of all kinds ranging from intimate forms of chamber theatre to comprehensive integrations of vast audiences with even vaster spectacles claimed the imaginations of some of the leading theorists of the time.

During the 1920s and 1930s, architect Walter Gropius, in collaboration with the theatre director Erwin Piscator, developed a proposal for a spatially adaptable theatre in Germany. In the same decades, the industrial and theatrical designer Norman Bel Geddes conceived a number of production-specific theatre designs in the United States. Although these as well as many other such projects seldom went beyond the sketch and model stage, their exhibition and publication throughout the world were influential in their time and served as inspiration for several nontraditional theatres built in the decades following World War II.

Questioning the validity of traditional theatre architecture led to reappraisals of the theatrical event. In turn, these reappraisals led to new approaches to theatrical presentation as well as new forms of theatres to accommodate them. A wealth of projects for multiform convertible theatres as well as production-specific environments encouraged visionary designers to think about possibilities for a radically new theatre architecture.

Chief among the multiform experiments was the 1927 large-capacity Gropius/Piscator "Totaltheater" that proposed within a single encompassing form the possibility of rotating part of the auditorium and converting mechanically from framed pictorial to central staging.

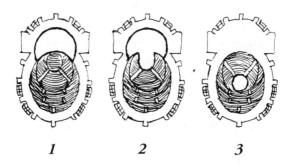

1   *2*   *3*

Plan number 1 illustrates an end stage joined to an oval auditorium in such a way that the stage seems to be embracing the audience rather than merely confronting it. Plan number 2 converts the down front seating section into a platform thrust that combines with the deep stage to physically link the performance area with the auditorium. Plan number 3 revolves the central seating area 180 degrees so that the platform arrives at the focus of a complete theatre-in-the-round.

Although the "Totaltheater" proposal itself was never executed, it did serve to influence aspects of a number of innovative built projects most notably the multiform Vivian Beaumont Theatre in New York City and the Loeb Drama Center at Harvard.

Prominent among production-specific proposals was a concept for an environment to accommodate an elaborate production scheme for a staging of Dante's Divine Comedy. *Conceived by scenic artist and industrial designer Norman Bel Geddes in the early 1930s, this project was widely publicized at the time of its appearance.*

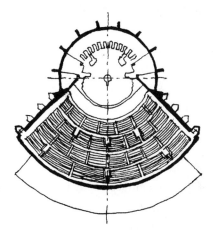

Monumental in scope and incorporating a permanent stage setting meant to support a cast of hundreds performing before an audience of thousands, Bel Geddes's conception seemed innovative and visually stimulating — at least in model form. Had it actually been built, however, it would most likely have dwarfed its human participants — actors as well as spectators — and violated acceptable standards of performance sight and sound.

Fanciful as many of these proposals were, there was nevertheless an underlying concern with the functional requirements of a theatrical event. Rather than concentrating energies on developing opulent visual embellishments for the auditorium and lobby areas, attention was paid to the dynamics of performance. To highlight this, emphasis was placed on the development of meaningful space in terms of simplified geometry. As a consequence, many such proposals relied on stripped-down modernist forms with a minimum of surface decoration to make their desired effects.

Aesthetics, liberated from a preoccupation with traditional concerns of what constitutes the essence of "beauty," was redefined in terms of how well a structure might perform relative to its intended use. Architectural method, in general, fueled by the theory of relativity and the concept of the space-time continuum, adopted the form-follows-function approach to design. In sum, the quality of architectural space was recognized to be of greater significance than the appearance of the elements that defined it. These widely accepted theories of architecture strongly influenced the design of theatres.

Intuition, based on functional analysis, became the acceptable way to go about developing workable theatres. Rather than prethinking results, this method encouraged the tracing of anticipated lines of function until an environment that could contain them would eventually reveal itself. This approach, typified by the work of Gropius and Bel Geddes, often produced startlingly original solutions that bore little resemblance to what previous cultures had thought of as appropriate theatres.

· · ·

Because the theatrical environment is essentially incomplete without the presence of the actors and audience in a performance situation, the planning of the structure must take the human potential very much into consideration. In design, this means analyzing and understanding the physical and psychological natures of the spectators as well as the performers and combining their separate realities into a form of environment that will support the heightened reality of a theatrical event.

The essence of the design of an auditorium lies in the functional analysis of the space in terms of the audience's seeing and hearing of the event and a similar analysis of the relationship of individual members of the audience to the audience as a whole. The essence of the design of stage space resides in the functional analysis of the characteristics of the potential performance. Resolving the relationship of these two aspects of a theatre — stage and auditorium — determines the degree of concentration that an audience can develop and sustain.

In the late 19th century, when naturalism in scenic design was the dominant force, the desire to create a complete reality for the stage environment caused the auditorium to be effectively divorced from the world of the performance. However, as time went on, it was seen that, no matter how convincing a replica of nature might be achieved on the stage, it was still accomplished by the most unnatural means — on a conventional platform framed by a conventional arch. As the ideal of naturalism began to wane, the inherent potential of the platform as a frankly stated support for performance once again came into its own.

By the early decades of the 20th century, it seemed most appropriate that, in order to recapture the essence of the great theatres of the past, the stage be once again expressed in terms of the traditional boards that actors had trod since the Middle Ages. It was thought that the floor of the stage should be frankly exposed in its naked carpentry and used as support for a space reserved primarily for acting, not for the illusions of scenic embellishment. The entrances and exits for this space should be clearly expressed and functional in terms of performance requirements, and the physical separation of the stage space from the auditorium should be minimized as much as possible.

On such a platform, it was expected that the performance, embodied in the movements of actors in space, would be reinforced by only the slightest and most subtle indications of scenic investiture. Instead, costumes, properties, and sound effects would contribute more significantly to the overall effect of the event. Bathed in the most expressive and responsive system of lighting yet available, this reconceived type of facility would surely result in performances unmatched for effectiveness in the whole history of the theatre.

It was with these expectations that the great theatricalist experiments of the early 20th century were undertaken. Such experiments assumed that the proper arena for the presentation of theatre could include the auditorium as well as the stage. The gilded frame of the Italian operatic tradition had to go. It was hoped that a return to the sort of bare platform that inspired the literary output of a Molière or a Shakespeare might once again rescue drama from the clutches of irrelevant distractions.

· · ·

Throughout the 1920s and 1930s, numerous experiments on the relationship of actors to audiences were conducted, most of them entirely abandoning the use of the proscenium arch in order to break down the audience's distance from the presentation. Theatrical events were once again presented with the audience all around them and sometimes the performers would even surround the audience. Stages were made to project into the middle of the auditorium. Sometimes they were constructed to hover over the heads of the spectators. Audiences were even made to sit within and around the area of the setting and had to mingle with the performers before, during, and after the performance. In this way, all physical separation could be blurred to the point where stage reality and audience participation could hardly be distinguished from one another. Experiments in merging performers and audiences influenced how intimately stages and auditoriums could relate to one another. Spatial unity rather than separation governed the staging of these performances.

In the 1930s, the Artistic Director of Moscow's Realistic Theatre Nikolai Okhlopkov rejected the isolation of the framed stage in favor of merging and melding performers and audiences within a single space.

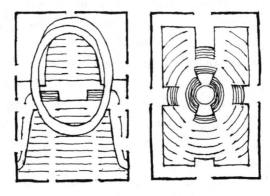

The diagram on the left shows an audience divided between stage and auditorium and facing a central playing area with ramps spiraling off from the platform to the sides and overhead.

The diagram on the right (above) illustrates an audience surrounding a central platform and in turn being surrounded by an encircling stage. In such a scheme all separation between performers and spectators is abolished.

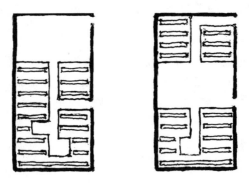

In the 1960s, similar experiments were revived at the Polish Theatre Laboratory by Jerzy Grotowski but this time on a far more intimate

scale. In small spaces with small casts and small audiences, an intense relationship among participants was established and maintained. The diagram on the left shows a space cleared for performance at one end of a room with performance paths winding through audience space. On the right the focus of the performance is more central, with the audience divided but still apt to be infiltrated by the performers. In yet other arrangements, audience and performers were so intricately interwoven that scant distinction could be made between the spheres of one or the other.

These experiments in the merging of actors and audiences, which were carried out with such fervor in the period between World War I and World War II, surfaced again in the 1950s and flourished in the laboratory theatres of the 1960s. In the theatre work of such innovators as Jerzy Grotowski, the spectators were made to actively identify with the performance action at close range and were often pressed into service to reinforce the event through direct participation. The effect of all this was to cancel out the traditional abyss between actors and spectators.

• • •

In the absence of a definitive concept to guide formal architectural solutions for 20th century theatrical environments, a series of schemes appeared that stressed a type of black-box enclosure. The black box provided seemingly unlimited flexibility. Within it might be created the entire range of imaginable actor/audience relationships. Such schemes featured totally flexible spaces unencumbered by permanent structural divisions.

The entire space could be adapted to the event so that audience seating would become just one more variable in the total production scheme.

A tabula rasa capable of accommodating limitless varieties of audience arrangement as well as performance staging became the mid-20th century ideal and challenge of those who wished to be able to control the event and its environment without physical restriction of any kind.

Generally speaking, this uncommitted architectural space or "black box" was modelled on the plan of a motion picture soundstage with technical equipment such as light and sound reinforcement located within a gridded ceiling. The floor was left free of physical encumbrance so that any arrangement of stage and auditorium was made possible.

In some more elaborate proposals, such as the various projects developed during the 1950s and 1960s by George Izenour at Yale, the basis of the design was a modular arrangement of seating sections and stage surfaces mounted on hydraulic lifts. Flexible as these schemes appeared to be, they were often deemed too uneconomical to maintain and, in most applications, were translated into simpler versions employing sets of moveable bleachers arranged in modular fashion on an open performance floor.

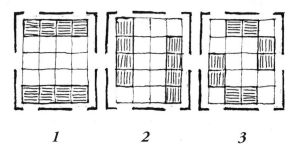

Typical arrangements of a black box might include (number 1) seating sections facing off against each other yielding a static central performance space, (number 2) sections asymmetrically placed to create a more dynamic stage form, or (number 3) clusters of seating arranged to contain or surround the action. In any case, the entire audience seldom shares a comparable view and, consequently, the overall impact of the performance may frequently seem diffuse.

Such complete freedom of choice in environmental manipulation places an unusually heavy burden on the director who must then be responsible not only for the arrangement of the performance areas but for the arrangement of the audience areas as well. Decisions relative to audience point of view are difficult to arrive at once one abandons the purely frontal relationship, since the entire audience will not be able to share a common impression of the event.

When performances are more ritualistic than theatrical, it is not as crucial that everyone perceive them in relatively the same way, since everyone is theoretically already acquainted with the ritual. However, since most modern dramatic expression cannot rely on a universally established social or philosophical frame of reference, it cannot be assumed that each member of an audience will understand and react to the dramatic presentation with the same mind-set. Therefore, each element of the production must be deliberately and fully revealed to each member of the audience equally in the course of the event.

· · ·

A strong influence on theatre design in the early 20th century was the rapid development of the motion picture as a dramatic medium. Movies demonstrated that long shots alternating with close-ups could give a far greater sense of urgency to a dramatic situation than the constant point of view experienced in a conventional legitimate theatre. This idea, too, encouraged experimentation in fragmenting an audience within a totally flexible environment. In fact, the very concept of the totally flexible space was probably suggested by the great hangarlike enclosures of the modern movie studios in which miracles of environmental manipulation could take place.

However, what was often overlooked in these live theatrical applications was that the dramatic impact of a film is made up of a skillful editing of individual shots all of which are recorded through the lens of a camera and transmitted to an audience as one totally defined work held within a rigid frame that surrounds the projection screen. Whether sitting near the screen or far, to the left or to the right, everyone in the movie audience experiences essentially the same movie. Within the totally flexible live theatrical environment there was established no such uniform frame of reference which could be shared by an entire audience. Some members of the audience had an entirely different theatrical experience from other members of the audience. There was no unified response, only a fragmented one.

The result was frequently an unsatisfactory experience for the spectators. Depending on their specific locations, some members of the audience at any given moment might be experiencing the equivalent of an extreme close-up of a particular action while others might be completely unaware of a dramatic element taking place in another part of the space. Such fragmentation would invariably have a deleterious impact on the total effect of the event.

The essential act of live theatre as opposed to film has actors and audience interfacing with one another at the precise moment of performance. If all elements of a production are not communicated to all the spectators simultaneously, the overall impact of the event will be blunted. Only experimentation that seriously considers the necessity for such unity of communication in theatrical presentation will have any lasting influence on the further evolution of live theatrical environments.

SEVEN

Continuation

As we evaluate the state of our contemporary theatre in an effort to preserve the evolution of live entertainment, it is clear that, no matter what innovations technology might have in store for us, the three fundamental principles of Focus, Platform, and Frame must in some combination or other continue to play a significant role in any further developments.

Every rational, humanistically based theatre from antiquity to the present has had to combine these three elements one way or another in order to achieve a workable actor/audience relationship appropriate to its time and social context. Human beings and their powers of interpretation and perception remain the measure in the creation of all things useful especially as far as theatres are concerned. Taming the technical aspects of theatre so they do not overwhelm the essential act of performance requires great skill. To the extent that it can successfully achieve this, theatre architecture can lay claim to the status of an art form.

As an art form reflective of society and attuned to its prevailing economics, the creation of any theatre must adopt a practical attitude toward accommodating its intended program. It should, of course, be planned to be able to withstand long-term economic pressure while still fostering the highest standards of contemporary production. But, even more importantly, it should never fail to embody an expression of the cultural aspirations of its time and make solid provision for the art that it is meant to house.

Art can provide an unparalleled opportunity for reinterpreting and giving shape to the confusions and ambiguities of day-to-day existence. Especially in theatre — an art form distinguished by its embodiment in human performance — a recasting of experience into a logical progression can present a welcome alternative to the comparative chaos of ordinary life.

It is this promise of order that can entice an audience, eager for form and meaning, to give their active attention to performers who, by means of their talent and training and their physical presence, can provide insights into the human condition. A theatre, governed by an awareness of so important a mission, can be a powerful medium for making sense of the apparently senseless.

As an emblem of the culture which spawns it, a theatre is fundamentally a facility for human interaction in which the material of life can be transformed into art. As such, it plays a pivotal role in giving significant shape to experience and should function with the highest possible degree of efficiency. It should allow an audience to observe and react, and it should permit a rehearsed event to take place without distortion. In order for a theatre to fulfill this obligation, it must be capable of bringing spectators and performers together in an intricate interrelationship that can unleash forces that neither side could achieve alone.

In the course of such interaction, performers (provided with material by writers and composers and directed or choreographed within specially designed stage environments) and an assembly of spectators are brought together within a structure that contains them both. The impulses that emanate from the platform must release in the audience an empathetic response sufficient to nourish the continuing interchange that is essential to the success of a live event.

It is important that the unique contributions of both actors and spectators be supported by theatre structures that can assist successful interaction. Unless, for example, performers feel confident that their efforts can be seen and heard by an entire audience, they will hardly appear at their best. If backstage facilities are inadequate or inefficient, there will be a deleterious effect on the mental attitudes they bring to their performances on stage.

Just as insecure and uncomfortable performers will be unable to give their best performances, individual members of an audience, inhibited by acoustical dead spots or faulty sight lines, will have difficulty coalescing into a responsive body capable of supporting the efforts being put forth from the stage. Unless the design of a theatre can permit both of these functions — the performing and the receiving — to fuse into lively and reciprocal interaction, the event will be limited in its emotional and intellectual potential.

As has been pointed out, this fusion of elements is among the most difficult and elusive problems to solve in all of architecture. Because the audience space must possess an integrity of its own as well as the capability of yielding this integrity to the created world of the stage at the moment of performance, it presents a formidable challenge in its design.

A successful audience arrangement is more than just the sum total of its scientifically coordinated sight lines and acoustics. It should possess a unique sense of place both before and after a performance. Its interior treatments should be capable of holding their own against the many lighting and sound equipment installations that must, because of production necessity, be located within the audience space itself. While having the chameleonlike ability to transform itself into a receptor for impulses coming from the stage during a given performance, it must still be able to preserve its identity as a safe and comfortable haven for its audience.

In deciding how large the capacity of a newly planned house should be, many factors must be taken into account. Among these are: location, relative real estate values, audience potential, whether one or more theatres of different sizes will be planned for a complex or whether the theatre will stand alone, and whether it will house self-generated productions or touring shows. For live performance, there are dimensional limitations on distance governing a satisfactory interaction of performers and audience and these parameters must not be exceeded. A methodical and thoughtfully conceived program, taking into account all of the above criteria, will yield individual answers to the question of a specific auditorium's appropriate size and shape.

．．．

The stage is a zone of high potential. Although essentially an empty space, it must be capable of accommodating the specific design elements of a particular event and of allowing them to function without physical hindrance of any kind. The created space of any production must be able to interface with the audience area in such a way that individual members of the audience will feel at one with the artistic intention. It is along the line of demarcation between the separate accommodations for performers and spectators that the resources of theatre architecture meet their greatest test.

The challenge lies in the fact that this line of demarcation must somehow be made to appear unobtrusive at the moment of performance even though in that location are to be found so many of the elements that make the event itself possible. The house curtain — if it exists — is here, the forestage is here, with a musical production the orchestra pit with an unobstructed view of the performance area for the conductor is here, the baffles that keep the onstage lighting from blinding the audience are here, the speakers that complement and reinforce the performance sound are here. And the physical structuring that permits the fusion of the two distinct worlds of audience and performers into one must somehow be accommodated here without calling undue attention to itself.

In any architectural solution for this zone of juxtaposition, important factors to be considered are the relative height of the platform to the viewing positions from first row to last, the shape of the auditorium relative to the shape of the stage, and the sight line and acoustic considerations that bind these two elements together. Each architectural program will require its individual solution. But as that solution is sought, the goal should be the same: the efficient and aesthetic synthesis between the two entities of performers and receivers.

· · ·

Because indoor theatres first made their appearance during the Renaissance and found their essential form in the ballroom and court theatres of the 17th and 18th centuries, the image of the proscenium house with its elaborately escutcheoned arch has persisted into our own time. Even though popular theatres of the 19th and 20th centuries with their larger capacities and more democratic arrangements favored galleries and, later, balconies over sumptuously appointed private boxes, vestiges of gilding, crystal, and plush still tend to dominate theatre interiors today.

Throughout our century, however, efforts have been made, especially in noncommercial situations, to democratize the theatre by stripping away the frames and flounces of an inherited baroque. The result has often been an exposure to view of hitherto concealed production equipment such as lights and speakers on stage as well as within the auditorium.

In an effort to solve all theatrical problems under one roof, some multiform completely adaptable theatres were developed. In these theatres many different configurations were possible — theatre-in-the-round, thrust, framed stage and all possibilities beyond and in between these. In many cases where the multiform theatre was embraced as the solution to all theatrical staging ideas, however, it was found that the theatre worked best in one particular configuration. And what had seemed to be totally adaptable eventually settled into one form or another, with the various potentials for changing shape remembered but neglected as time went on.

In an effort to unite all elements into one zone, the audience has often been absorbed into space traditionally reserved for performers. As noted before, in some newer theatres long-held conventional separations were discarded for the sake of novelty or for the sake of revolutionizing the event in hopes of making it seem more relevant to contemporary audiences.

In the process of experimentation, many values considered to be fundamental to the theatrical event can be lost. If an audience is so scattered around the playing area that the actors are confused about where to aim their performances, the performances will be less effective. If actors cannot encompass the assembled spectators at a glance and direct their performances with the assurance that each and every member of the audience will be receiving the same impulse at the same time, a diminishing of tension and a slowing of pace results. When actors have to wrestle with the form of a stage and its relationship to an audience, it lessens the spontaneity and effectiveness of their performances. When that happens, even innovative directors can find themselves preferring to re-embrace the greater focus of the framed stage in order to be better able to control the nuance and effect of the event.

But experimentation — even if it does not result in an immediately perceptible evolution of architectural form — does have its value. It questions accepted beliefs and exposes possible fallacies in logic. It encourages an irreverence that can lead to a more adventurous approach in staging techniques. It reasserts the notion that the theatrical presentation, unfolding in the Now, has the responsibility to explore the contemporary in design and theory, form and content. By doing so, it might even inspire a revitalization of dramatic literature.

Free experimentation based on instinct and a knowledge of past achievements can provide important insights into possible further evolutionary steps. Along the way, experimental theatres that are actually built, no matter what their strengths or weaknesses, can provide practical laboratories for testing the boundaries of theory. Beginning with an understanding of the three basic principles of theatre design (Focus, Platform, and Frame), performers, directors, designers, as well as co-operating spectators can explore the possibilities of new forms in order to shed light on further developments.

• • •

Architecture has always benefited from having to grapple with contemporary problems, thereby developing forms that truly reflect and epitomize the aspirations of any particular age. Theatre architecture, for its part, challenged by the necessity of merging two seemingly antithetical zones of human activity into an entity greater than the sum of its parts, can be a true reflection of its time and place and can provide a litmus test for the state of the arts of both theatre and architecture.

The ultimate test of any theatre — from the simplest arrangement of boards and benches to the most sophisticated and technically developed performance environment — lies in its ability to bring together the living presence of actor and audience in ways that can yield high levels of theatrical excitement. The degree to which such excitement can be generated and maintained in performance is, of course, directly dependent on the personal resources of the active participants, but encouraging and supporting their potential is the mandate of those who design their physical environments.

If the living theatre is to hold its own against encroaching simulations and be able to successfully survive into the new millennium, environments will have to be provided that can foster effective actor/audience relationships in a contemporary context. What is planned and what is built should be based on an understanding of present day needs in the light of significant past achievements. From such understanding can come enlightened and inspired solutions that will encourage and facilitate the further evolution of theatre so it may continue to hold its place as the liveliest of the lively arts.

Afterword

As an architect committed to the cause of accommodating live performance, I have attempted, in the preceding chapters, to identify and analyze the particular elements that should concern anyone involved in the development of theatres.

Focus, Platform, and Frame, as I have indicated, are the three guiding principles upon which all such designs should be based. Since without a doubt the theatrical event is the reason for the whole undertaking, it is the task of the architect to insure that these particular elements contribute to the design in the most efficacious manner.

Whenever I find myself in an unoccupied theatre, I attempt to try out its sight lines from as wide a variety of seating locations as possible to see if they all converge on a point in space which will form the focus for any production that might be installed there. This focus should, if properly established, hover somewhere above the platform upon which a production might rest.

Walking onto the stage, I am drawn to seek out the platform's center in order to be able to observe the extent of the auditorium from the point of view of the performer. From this vantage point, one can also survey the locations from which will emanate the atmospheric enhancements — including the light sources that will illuminate and enframe the physical production. It is through this enframement that the audience will experience the event and will be able to relate to the environment of the performance.

The quality of these provisions will determine to a great degree just how successful any event staged there might be. If all of these devices can function in relational harmony, the experience of both performers and audience will be mutually gratifying.

In the best theatres, the event's the thing and the structure that contains it will relinquish its character at the moment of performance. The essential handiwork of the architect, if it is well conceived, will seem to have vanished in the service of the particular production, but its functional effectiveness will be keenly felt by everyone involved, performers and audience alike.

For the architect, the act of completing a theatre may prove to be an ego-bruising experience since the greater the architect's achievement, the less of a direct impact the appearance of the building will probably make on its intended public. Since the theatre's true excellence lies in its ability to selflessly enhance an event, the impressions that an audience takes away with it should most certainly be dominated by the effect of the event itself.

But gratifications can still exist. During the planning process, there is no moment more heady than the one in which all the elements of a program come together and the architect can visualize for the first time the potential of performers working with unfettered delight and audiences perceiving this and reacting with full enthusiasm. Conceiving appropriate spaces around the motivations and physical demands of those who will be involved with the presentation and those whose role it will be to react to it is the province, privilege, and reward of the theatre architect.

And if, when the theatre is finally operational, the performers leave the stage flushed with satisfaction both with their performance and the support that the facility has given them in achieving it, and the audience emerges in a state of fulfillment, the architect can derive satisfaction from the knowledge that the considerable efforts leading up to this moment have resulted in a successful realization.

All design that responds to human need and reflects the aspirations of its time transcends surface decoration and can claim the right to being called architecture. That a theatre might be considered to be an essentially utilitarian structure should in no way diminish its aesthetic value. In fact, the degree to which it appears to be self-effacing determines its excellence as a work of art.

A theatre, perhaps more than any other building type, must clearly express its functional "modernity" — its appropriateness to its time and place — no matter what stylistic veneer it may come wrapped in. If its outer forms can define and reflect its spatial reality, so much the better. But, in any event, it must work for its intended purpose — the melding of performers and spectators into an interactive entity. It must achieve for them what neither category of participant can achieve alone. It must celebrate the human spirit. It must elevate and enlighten. It must transfix and transform.

This may seem to be a heavy burden for a structure devoted merely to entertainment to have to bear. In reality, much more is involved. Providing the physical setting within which the highest levels of human skill and interpretation may be achieved and communicated to an assembled audience is what is truly at stake. And this communication, being live, can exist only at the moment of creation. So the characteristics of the container of the event are crucial to the event's very existence.

In a world increasingly dominated by electronic simulation and its tendency toward isolating individuals within their own personal spheres, live performance is at risk of becoming less and less central to everyday life. For this trend to continue unchecked would ultimately have disastrous effects on the human condition.

The provision of facilities for live theatre is important for all of the above reasons and demands the best: the best programming, the best site selection, and, above all, the best — most appropriately responsive, most *modern* — architecture in order to enhance the quality of the presentations that it is theatre architecture's unique privilege to nurture and support.